All Color World of
AIRCRAFT

All Color World of
AIRCRAFT

David Mondey

Contents

Jacket: The Red Arrows jet formation
squadron of the Royal Air Force.
Endpapers: A commercially sponsored
aerobatic team.
Title page: The Boeing P26-A entered service
with the USAAC in 1931.
This page: USAF jet fighters in formation.

First published 1978 by Octopus Books Limited
59 Grosvenor Street, London W1

© 1978 Octopus Books Limited
ISBN 0 7064 0707 5

Produced by Mandarin Publishers Limited
22a Westlands Road, Quarry Bay, Hong Kong

Printed in Hong Kong

The beginnings

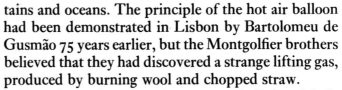

On 21 November 1783 came the first limited realization of man's long held desire to fly above the earth. On that day, in Paris, a hot air balloon designed and built by the brothers Étienne and Joseph Montgolfier carried Pilâtre de Rozier and the Marquis d'Arlandes on an 8 km (5 mile) flight across the French city. The desire to achieve the ability to travel through the air as freely as birds do had not evolved merely as a form of exploration, but because man had also realized that such a capability would permit him to travel without difficulty over natural barriers such as rivers, mountains and oceans. The principle of the hot air balloon had been demonstrated in Lisbon by Bartolomeu de Gusmão 75 years earlier, but the Montgolfier brothers believed that they had discovered a strange lifting gas, produced by burning wool and chopped straw.

Ten days after that first manned flight, J.A.C. Charles, accompanied by one of the Robert brothers who had helped construct his balloon, recorded in France the first manned flight—one of 43 km (27 miles)—in a hydrogen filled balloon. This was similar to a modern gas filled balloon; but whenever they

Far left: The Montgolfier brothers' hot air balloon which carried men in free flight for the first time in history. Left: An early gas filled balloon in flight. Above: A considerable problem for pioneer balloonists was producing hydrogen gas to inflate the balloon.

have flown, balloons are controlled by the wind, not by their occupants. It was essential that the pilot should be able to steer his chosen vehicle, and this requirement led to the development of airships.

The first of these to be considered an almost practical vehicle was that built by Charles Renard and Arthur Krebs in France, and this flew just over 100 years after the first hydrogen balloon. It led to the construction of such remarkable vessels as the British R.34 and Germany's world encircling *Graf Zeppelin*. By the time of the disaster to the Zeppelin *Hindenburg* in 1937 however, engineers had learned how to build heavier than air aircraft of far superior performance.

Long before the first men rose victoriously into the sky in a Montgolfier balloon, earlier generations of brave—or foolhardy—experimenters had tried to achieve flight in a variety of ways. Their ideas included wing membranes strapped between arms and legs with which to attempt gliding flight; wings attached to arms and legs so that they could try to fly in a birdlike manner; and odd looking machines driven by paddles and sails. None were successful.

Yet during these early years some vital ideas had been expressed and some of the first heavier than air craft had flown. These latter devices included the kite, invented in China some 1000 years before Christ, the first frail rotating-wing toys, and the introduction of rockets. In Italy Leonardo da Vinci (1452–1519) had designed a model helicopter, and an ornithopter

(flapping-wing aircraft) which he believed could be powered by a man's muscles. Two hundred years later a fellow Italian, Giovanni Borelli, proved that man would be unable to fly by muscle power alone. What was needed by all of the would-be fliers was a compact, lightweight source of power. Until this was discovered, their dreams of free flight would not be realized.

The sport of ballooning grew rapidly, and this limited success in achieving some form of flight acted as a spur to man's search. In addition, at this moment in aviation history the English baronet, Sir George Cayley, began to express important and fundamental findings that would exert considerable influence on the development of heavier than air craft. They included the first design for a fixed-wing aircraft of 'modern' configuration (1799); the first flight of a stable model glider (1804); the first appreciation that wing dihedral conferred lateral stability (1808); and in 1809 the first flight of a manned glider, investigation into streamlining, and the realization that a cambered upper wing surface would give more lift than one with a flat surface. Little wonder that Cayley is regarded as 'the father of aerial navigation'.

During the remaining years of the 19th century further discoveries provided the other pieces of the puzzle which when fitted together at the beginning of the 20th century were sufficient to enable men to make the first tentative flights in heavier than air powered aircraft. The first of these was the invention

in 1860 by Étienne Lenoir, in France, of the gas engine, the world's first internal combustion engine. This was to lead to the development in 1876 of the four stroke petrol engine by the German N.A. Otto, and of the world's first practical petrol engine by the German Gottlieb Daimler in 1885.

Other contributions came from W.S. Henson, who published in London his design for an 'Aerial Steam Carriage', which though never built represented the first propeller driven aircraft of modern monoplane configuration (1843); the successful flight of Cayley's third full size glider, which carried his coachman across a small valley (1853); the first successful flight of a powered model aeroplane in France, a clockwork driven monoplane built by Félix du Temple (1857); and in 1874 the first recorded take-off of a full size manned and powered version of the same aircraft. Launched down an inclined ramp at Brest, du Temple's aeroplane made only a brief hop, but it was the first significant and practical step forward. Ten years later, in July 1884, a second powered man-carrying aeroplane was launched similarly, down a ramp, and it also failed to achieve more than a brief hop. This was the steam powered monoplane built by Russia's Alexander Mozhaiski, and piloted by I.N. Golubev. Then, on 9 October 1890, Clement Ader's

Left: A model in the QANTAS collection of Félix du Temple's hot air powered aeroplane. Above: An airworthy replica of the Bristol 'Box-kite', of which 78 were built by the British & Colonial Aeroplane Company at Bristol, from 1910.

steam powered *Éole* became the world's first full size manned aeroplane to leave the ground under its own power. *Éole* made only a very short flight, of about 55 m (150 ft), but it appeared at first that France had gained a significant lead.

The more thoughtful pioneers realized that until a suitable power plant became available, their time would be employed most valuably in learning more about the theory and practice of flight. Foremost of these pioneers was Otto Lilienthal, a German who built a series of superb gliders which he flew most successfully. Of even greater importance was the fact that Lilienthal recorded very carefully the results of his experiments and flights, so that others might benefit from his experience. His work inspired two other pioneer designers and builders of gliders: Percy Pilcher in Britain, and Octave Chanute in America. Chanute collected the available literature on aviation which he published in a classic work: *Progress in Flying Machines*. This book, and Octave Chanute himself, did much to spur the American brothers

Orville and Wilbur Wright in their attempts to create a practical powered aircraft. The Wright brothers were nearly beaten in the attempt to achieve powered flight by fellow American Samuel Pierpont Langley. When his *Aerodrome* failed at the second attempt to become airborne, on 8 December 1903, the Wrights had a clear field. Thus, on 17 December 1903, at Kill Devil Hills near Kitty Hawk, North Carolina, Orville made the world's first powered, sustained and controlled flight of just 12 seconds.

Orville's flight was not the only one made on that historic day. Three others followed, with the brothers taking it in turn to pilot the *Flyer*. On the last flight of the day, Wilbur remained airborne for 59 seconds, in which time the frail aircraft had covered a distance of 260 m (852 ft). But this was not to prove the success story of 1903, in fact the world remained unaware that man had achieved powered flight until the Brazilian Alberto Santos-Dumont recorded the first official flight in Europe in his No 14 *bis*. Little more than a hop of 61 m (200 ft), it was witnessed by about a thousand spectators, officially timed and photographed. This was the flight that took the headlines, made on 23 October 1906, nearly three years after the triumph at Kitty Hawk.

From that moment, however, the pace of development began to accelerate. In April 1907 the Frenchman, Louis Blériot, built and tested—unsuccessfully—his No 5 monoplane, but by mid-January 1908, Henry Farman in France had recorded the first

Above: A model, also from the QANTAS collection, of one of Otto Lilienthal's gliders. Beautifully proportioned, and made of peeled willow wands covered with waxed linen, Lilienthal made thousands of flights in gliders like these. Right: A replica of A.V. Roe's triplane, the first all British heavier than air craft designed, built and flown by a Briton.

circular flight of 1 km (0.62 miles) in his Voisin-Farman biplane. And in August of that same year Wilbur Wright began a series of demonstration flights in France which proved how advanced was the Wright *Flyer A* by comparison with European designs; on 21 September he made a flight which lasted for more than 1½ hours. In the following year, on 13 July, A.V. Roe became the first Briton to fly an all British aircraft, the Roe 1 triplane.

Twelve days after A.V. Roe's first successful, if tentative flight, the Frenchman Louis Blériot gave the entire world food for thought by crossing the English Channel, from Les Baraques, near Calais, to Dover. His flight, of 36½ minutes' duration, in the Blériot XI monoplane, gave rise to the first serious realization of the aeroplane's potential as a weapon of war. No longer could any nation rely on such natural barriers as the sea for its defence, nor could it assume that its navy would be able to take any useful action that would deny an aircraft free access to its mainland.

Blériot's flight had not been without event. The major cause for concern came from the 18.6 kW (25 hp) three cylinder engine which powered his monoplane. Half-way over the Channel it began to overheat, and but for the extra cooling provided by a fortuitous shower of rain, Blériot might have failed. This incident emphasizes the main problem which beset these first aviation pioneers. The power output of most engines was barely sufficient to maintain flying speed, for one must remember that these early aircraft were far from being aerodynamically efficient. The result was that most engines overheated fairly quickly, and as soon as this happened engine power fell off, often making a forced landing inevitable.

The engines then in use were of two main types: big and heavy inline engines which derived from the automobile industry, or radial engines which had evolved for aircraft use, but which suffered from overheating because of inadequate aircooling. In 1907 Frenchman Laurent Seguin and his brother devoted their engineering skill to develop a new kind of power plant which would eliminate the weaknesses of these types, and introduced a rotary engine. This had a crankshaft that was, in effect, attached to the airframe,

and around which the crankcase, cylinders and propeller rotated as one. The cylinders, turning through the air, solved the cooling problem, and the mass of the engine ensured smooth running at low throttle openings. This was the power plant which gave a new surge to the development of aviation. By 1912 the Seguins were marketing a series of six Gnome engines, ranging from 37–119 kW (50–160 hp). And as a mark of the progress that had been made, it is worth recording that at the beginning of 1912 French aircraft held the world speed record of 133.14 km/h (82.73 mph); had flown a distance of 722.92 km (449.2 miles) in a closed circuit; and had climbed to a height of 3910 m (12,828 ft).

By the end of the first decade of powered flight there had been almost miraculous progress, as if that first flight of the Wright brothers had made a breach in some invisible barrier through which a torrent of pent-up genius and inventiveness was now flowing. A Peruvian, Georges Chavez, had crossed the Alps in a Blériot monoplane; the first official air mail flight had been made in India; C.S. Rolls, of Rolls-Royce fame,

had completed a non-stop double crossing of the English Channel; the first non-stop flight between London and Paris had been made in a Blériot monoplane; in France Henri Fabre had successfully flown the world's first seaplane; Igor Sikorsky, in Russia, had completed and flown the world's first four-engine aircraft, the 28 m (92 ft) wingspan *Bolshoi*; and in Germany there was being created quietly the largest military air force in the world.

It had been inevitable, from the earliest days of powered flight, that the military use of aircraft would not be long deferred. Indeed, as early as August 1909 the United States Army had acquired its first aircraft. In 1910 the American pioneer, Glenn Curtiss, had dropped dummy bombs on the outline of a battleship, and on 22 October 1911 the Italians made the first use of an aeroplane for aerial reconnaissance. This role of reconnaissance was the primary one envisaged for the aeroplane when World War 1 broke out in 1914.

Below: A replica, in appropriate setting, of Louis Blériot's Channel-crossing type XI monoplane.

Fighter aircraft 1914-1938

In 1914, Germany had the largest air force in the world, comprising about 260 aircraft, most of which were intended to fulfil a reconnaissance role. France had about 160 aircraft but, despite inferiority in numbers, had an advanced aviation industry that was not only to prove capable of producing steadily improving aircraft to meet the needs of its own fighting services, but was also able to build them in sufficient quantity to supply a fair percentage of the requirements of its allies. Britain had managed to supply 63 aircraft to equip its Royal Flying Corps in France, and their pilots had flown them across the Channel during the period 13–15 August 1914.

Prior to the war most army commanders had shown little interest in the aeroplane. They would agree that it was a useful means of carrying urgent messages, and

that subject to suitable weather it might prove to be a useful observation platform. And because this attitude prevailed, the 500 plus aircraft which Britain, France and Germany had mustered at the beginning of the war were, in the main, intended for reconnaissance. It was very quickly discovered that they were invaluable in this role; not only providing an army commander with a frequently updated picture of the enemy's dispositions, supplies, and the movement of reinforcements, they also demonstrated their ability to direct artillery to give new standards of accuracy

Below: A replica of the Curtiss JN–4, primary mount of America's postwar barnstormers. Above right: A replica of the Fokker Dr I triplane as flown by 'Red Baron', Manfred von Richthofen. Below right: German Pfalz D XII single-seat two-bay biplane fighter.

lenging their supremacy. First was Geoffrey de Havilland's D.H.2, built by the Aircraft Manufacturing Co., and which had a forward firing Lewis gun. This latter capability came as the result of the aircraft's 'pusher' configuration, meaning that the engine and propeller were mounted behind the pilot. The second British aircraft able to meet the Fokkers on equal terms was the Royal Aircraft Factory F.E.2b, also of pusher configuration. Neither had been designed specifically to meet the problems posed by the Fokkers with their forward firing machine guns; rather, they had been built in quantity at just the right moment in time—so far as the Allies were concerned. France contributed the Nieuport XI, a fast and manoeuvrable biplane of conventional tractor layout, that is with its engine and propeller mounted at the forward end of the airframe. It was not equipped with interrupter gear, instead its machine gun was mounted on the upper surface of the upper wing, in a central

position, so that its bullets passed clear of the spinning propeller blades.

The first allied scouting aircraft with interrupter gear was the Bristol Scout D, fitted initially with Vickers-Challenger gear, but it was not long before the combat aircraft of both sides were so equipped as routine.

The choice of the name 'Scout' for this little Bristol biplane is interesting because it emphasizes the role that had developed for a scout aircraft as the tactics of aerial warfare began to emerge. The need to deny your own airspace to the enemy was soon realized, but the reconnaissance role of the aeroplane was so important that it became necessary to ensure, so far as possible, that the observation machines were adequately guarded by aircraft which could scout ahead and around to drive off hostile aeroplanes.

It was not long before 'scouts' became 'fighters', and as the war progressed their numbers increased

Above: A dog fight, depicted by N.C. Arnold.

rapidly. When the fighter/escorts of one side met those of the enemy, carrying out exactly the same task for their colleagues, battle was joined, and aerial warfare over the Western Front during the latter years of World War 1 was highlighted by furious 'dog fights' between opposing fighters. From such engagements emerged the 'aces' whose names have become a colourful part of aviation's history: men such as America's Rickenbacker, Belgium's Coppens, Bishop and Collishaw from Canada, Fonck and Guynemer of France, von Richthofen and Udet from Germany, the Italian Baracca, and Mannock and McCudden of the United Kingdom. These, of course, were the leading aces; there were many others, some of whom made important contributions to the tactics of war, and in particular one should note the two Germans Boelcke and Immelmann. The former was the first to advocate a striking force of fighter aircraft, while the latter was concerned with combat tactics and is remembered to this day by the manoeuvre known as the 'Immelmann turn'.

As the numbers of aircraft involved in 'dog fights' increased, and their speed and agility improved, it became necessary that pilots involved in these clashes should be able easily to identify both friendly and hostile aircraft. This led to more extensive use of insignia that would make recognition easy, and aircraft, especially those of German squadrons, became painted in brilliant colours and patterns. Typical was Manfred von Richthofen's Fokker Triplane, painted bright crimson, so that the 'Red Baron' and his squadron could be seen and recognized at a glance. This ease of identification was perhaps more important than is generally appreciated, for sudden death could come from an area other than the sky. In the kind of trench warfare that had developed on the Western Front, it was realized that aircraft could add to the misery of ground troops, strafing their fixed positions with a hail of machine gun bullets which, even if they did not decimate the occupants of the trenches, were most effective in making them keep their heads down at a tactical moment. Not surprisingly, ground forces tended to fire small arms at aircraft which came too close, and any means which could assist identification of friendly aircraft was worthwhile.

There was another area of offensive operations in which allied fighter aircraft brought about a complete change of ideas. At the beginning of the war Germany believed that her lighter than air Zeppelin airships would be able to make devastating attacks on Britain, even though the Kaiser had decreed they should be deployed only against military targets. However, due to the problems of navigating such craft with any real degree of accuracy, it was inevitable that attacks on non-military targets would occur, causing death and injury to a number of civilians. By the casualty stan-

dards of World War 2 they were little more than incidents, but there was sharp reaction to such attacks on Britain, and measures were taken to deal with the menace of the Zeppelins. In fact, it was the machine gun equipped fighter aircraft, spitting out a hail of incendiary bullets, that marked their end. Almost a third of the military Zeppelins were shot down and about a similar proportion were lost by bombing action or accidents. When on 5 August 1918 the pride of the German navy, Zeppelin L.70, was shot down by Major Cadbury and Captain Leckie, flying a de Havilland D.H.4 patrol seaplane, it marked the end of Zeppelin activity. In command of the L.70 on that fateful day was Fregatten Kapitän Peter Strasser, Chief of the German Naval Airship Division, and the driving force behind the service. His death in the wreckage of the L.70 brought the end of military airships.

Mention of naval forces reminds us that the aeroplane was not exclusively a servant of land based troops. Naval commanders had appreciated at a very early stage in aviation history that such a device would, when adapted for maritime service, provide eyes which could see beyond the horizon. Frenchman Henri Fabre had flown the world's first successful hydro-aeroplane (seaplane) in March 1910. America and Britain both recorded seaplane flights in the following year, but the early Hydro-Aeroplane Meetings at Monaco and the first Schneider Trophy Contests speeded the development of practical seaplanes. The fact that they must take off from and land on water limited considerably the early military use of such aircraft, for in addition to the fact that a fairly calm sea was necessary for their operation, it meant that the ship which carried such long range eyes had to stop both to launch and recover its seaplane.

These shortcomings were appreciated very quickly and as early as January 1911 a landing on and take-off from the American cruiser USS *Pennsylvania* was demonstrated by Eugene Ely flying a Curtiss biplane. The *Pennsylvania* was at anchor for both demonstrations, but just over a year later a Short biplane amphibian was flown off the British battleship HMS *Hibernia* while it steamed at a speed of 19.15 km/h (10.5 knots). The potential of an aircraft carrier was appreciated and it was but a matter of time before such vessels became reality. The first true aircraft carriers, intended for the operation of landplanes from a flight deck, was Britain's HMS *Furious*, and in August 1917 the first deck landing on a ship under way was recor-

Above right: The Gloster Gladiator was the first RAF fighter to carry four machine guns.
Right: Another view of a Pfalz D XII replica. Some pilots preferred it to the Fokker D.VII.
Overleaf: On the ground and (inset) in flight a fine replica of the Sopwith Aviation Company's famous Pup.

The Scout Experimental (SE) 5a was the Royal Aircraft Factory's best design of the World War I period, and was bettered in results as a fighter only by the superlative Sopwith Camel. In design philosophy, the two standard fighters of the 1917–18 period were poles apart. The SE-5a (derived from the lower-powered SE-5) was a very robust, powerful machine, and enjoyed its combat success as a result of its speed, strength and

stability as a gun platform rather than because of its agility. Deliveries of the SE-5a began in June 1917, and a total of 5,205 machines of the SE-5/5a family was built. Plans for the Curtiss company to build another 1,000 in the United States were cancelled after the war.

Royal Aircraft Factory SE-5a

SPECIFICATIONS

Type	single-seat fighter
Engine	200-hp Hispano-Suiza, 220 hp Hispano-Suiza, 200 hp Wolseley W.4A Viper, 200 hp Wolseley Adder, or 200 hp Sunbeam Arab (all 8-cylinder liquid-cooled inlines)
Armament	one fixed, synchronized .303-inch Vickers machine gun and one .303-inch Lewis machine gun, plus four 25-pound Cooper bombs
Speed	126 mph at 10,000 feet
Climb	13 minutes 15 seconds to 10,000 feet
Ceiling	17,500 feet
Endurance	$2\frac{1}{4}$ hours
Weight	1,531 pounds (empty) 2,048 pounds (loaded)
Span	26 feet 7.4 inches
Length	20 feet 11 inches
Height	9 feet 6 inches

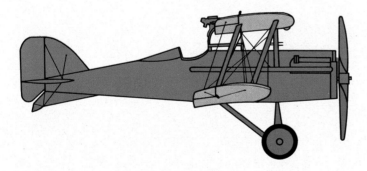

ded by a Sopwith Pup flown on to the *Furious* by Squadron Commander Dunning.

Operation from vessels at sea, however, was not the main activity of naval aircraft during World War 1. The majority of military aircraft operated by naval forces were used in a reconnaissance role, but an early realization that an aeroplane might launch a torpedo with deadly effect led to the development of aircraft and weapons for this purpose.

As World War 1 neared its end large squadrons of fighter aircraft were in service with the combatant nations. France had built great numbers of steadily improving Nieuport fighters, and the SPAD Company had developed some superb machines which were built in large quantities for their own air force as well as for its allies. The SPAD XIII, entering service in May 1917, totalled more than 8400 aircraft before production ended. The best fighter to be produced by

Britain's Royal Aircraft Factory was the S.E.5a, a machine in which many of the allied aces won their fame, but few will deny the Sopwith Pup and Camel their unique place in aviation history. The Pup, despite its small size, was a giant in combat and Manfred von Richthofen commented that it was superior to the aircraft of his unit. Its two great qualities were extremely sensitive and responsive controls, plus the ability to stay in contact in combat without losing height. The slightly larger Camel, which it is claimed destroyed almost 1300 enemy aircraft, was remarkable not only for its agility, but also for the effectiveness of its belt-fed twin Vickers machine guns.

Germany could not allow the Allies to gain control

In terms of enemy aircraft destroyed (1,294), the Sopwith Camel was the most successful fighter of World War I, its only rival for the title of the best fighter of the war being the Fokker D-VII. Unlike the contemporary SE-5a, the Camel (developed from the Pup) was designed with extreme manoeuvrability in

mind: the positioning of most of the heavy items of equipment (engine, fuel, guns, ammunition and pilot) in the front seven feet of the fuselage ensured this, although it took an experienced pilot to get the best out of the Camel. The F.1 Camel entered service in the middle of 1917, and was soon joined by a ship-board version, the 2F.1, which had a single Vickers gun and a Lewis gun on the top wing. A total of 5,490 Camels was built.

Sopwith Camel

SPECIFICATIONS

Type	single-seat fighter
Engine	110 hp Clerget 9Z, 130 hp Clerget 9B, 140 hp Clerget 9Bf, 110 hp Le Rhone, 100 hp Gnome Monosoupape, 150 hp Bentley BR1, or 170 hp Le Rhone 9R (all 9-cylinder rotaries)
Armament	two fixed, synchronized .303-inch Vickers machine guns (or two .303-inch Lewis machine guns on the night fighter version)
Speed	104½ mph at 10,000 feet
Climb	11 minutes 45 seconds to 10,000 feet
Ceiling	19,000 feet
Endurance	2½ hours
Weight	962 pounds (empty) 1,482 pounds (loaded)
Span	28 feet
Length	18 feet 9 inches
Height	8 feet 6 inches

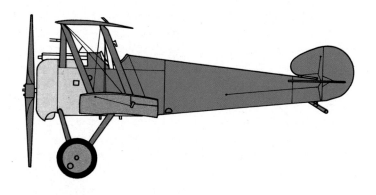

of the airspace above the Western Front, and in 1917 launched a competition to develop a military scout/fighter that, hopefully, would regain the initiative. When the competing aircraft were judged, in January 1918, the Fokker D.VII, designed by Reinhold Platz, was an easy winner and when introduced on the Western Front in the early summer of 1918 it demonstrated immediately its capabilities. Once again the Allies were confronted by an aircraft that was able to out-perform their best fighters, but fortunately for them its introduction came too late in the war to have a significant influence on its outcome. Its potential was well understood, however, for the Armistice documents drawn up by the Allies in November 1918 specified that all aircraft of the D.VII type must be

handed over to the French or British authorities.

The 'War to end Wars' was over, and it has been accepted fairly generally that the stresses of war had developed the frail toy of the sporting fraternity into a robust and efficient aircraft which, with a return to peace, would be readily adaptable to provide air travel for the peoples of the world. This vision was rather optimistic, however, for the Fokker D.VII only had a top speed of about 188 km/h (117 mph), powered by a Mercedes engine of 119 kW (160 hp). Yet the Royal Aircraft Factory S.E.4 biplane, built in 1914, had a maximum speed of 217 km/h (135 mph) with an engine of the same power. It is undeniable, however, that there had been a significant improvement in engine power and reliability. The somewhat tentative 74.5 kW (100 hp) engines of 1914 had given way to such as the Rolls-Royce Eagle of 194 kW (260 hp), and here is the key to postwar progress.

Pioneer passenger airliners

Farsighted men, keen to speed the development of civil airlines that would carry people on business, and pleasure, flights over intercontinental routes, had been busy making plans while the war was still in progress. In Britain, George Holt Thomas had registered Aircraft Transport and Travel Ltd as early as 5 October 1916; in the following year Pierre Latécoère in France was planning how he might achieve a service between his native land and Morocco as the first stepping-stone in a service that would one day link France and South America.

They, and many others with similar ideas, were way ahead of their time. They duly initiated air services of a kind, only to discover that the 'man in the street' was not yet ready to accept air travel. Despite the amount of activity in the air during the war, there was still a general feeling that it was a somewhat hazardous means of getting from A to B, even assuming that one could afford the cost. Only people that we would class as rich could afford a London–Paris return fare in excess of £30 (equivalent to about £200 in today's currency), and it became clear even to those who could afford it that, for one reason or another, the services were far from reliable. The first need was to demonstrate to the public that flight was safe, and to this end various efforts were made to sponsor flights which would gain widespread publicity. In Britain the *Daily Mail* newspaper, which had done much to encourage aviation from its earliest days, offered a prize of £10,000 for the first non-stop flight across the North Atlantic. A similar prize was offered by the Australian Government for a first flight from England to Australia.

At 8.40 a.m. on the morning of 15 June 1919, a Vickers Vimy nosed-over in a bog at Clifden, Eire; Captain John Alcock and Lieutenant Arthur Whitten Brown had just completed the first non-stop crossing of the North Atlantic from Newfoundland, in a flying time of 16 h 27 min. Just less than five months later, on 12 November, Australian brothers Captain Ross Smith and Lieutenant Keith Smith took off from Hounslow, Middlesex in another Vimy, en route to Darwin, Australia, where they landed just under 28

days later. All four of these men were knighted subsequently for their achievements.

The flight which captured the imagination of people all over the world, however, and which more than any other brought the realization that at last flying was a safe means of travel for the ordinary man, was that achieved by American Charles Lindbergh in 1927. Taking off from Long Island, New York, in a single engine Ryan monoplane—*Spirit of St Louis*—on 20 May, he flew the North Atlantic alone, non-stop, landing at Paris 33 h 39 min later after a flight of 5810 km (3610 miles). His reception was tumultuous; many wondered how this slim, shy American had found the stamina to endure the strain of such an epoch making flight.

Charles Lindbergh had grown up with aviation, and was in fact one of the tough, experienced pilots, who had helped to establish the US Air Mail Service. This had become an integral part of the American way of life, and in 1923 the service had carried close on 70 million letters. It had blazoned air lanes across the United States, created a pool of skilled pilots, and had established trails of beacon lights so that the mails could travel by day and night. This was the sound foundation upon which the American airlines could build when they got under way in 1927. Strangely, the country which had led the world in powered flight, was slow to capitalize on the enormous potential rewards for the inaugurators of the first domestic airlines. European countries had been quicker off the mark, but most began with a proliferation of small companies which seemed to run out of money and enthusiasm at about the same time. In Britain, for example, where four companies had pinched and scraped for survival from early postwar days, the Government promised aid to buy new aircraft and equipment if they would combine as a national airline. Thus was born Imperial Airways. By much the same progression of events the great national airlines such as Air France, KLM, Lufthansa and Sabena emerged; all have survived to the present day except that Imperial Airways, via British Overseas Airways Corporation, has become British Airways.

Above: Kenneth McDonough's fine painting captures the feeling of the early 1920s as this Handley Page W.8b crosses Plough Lane, Croydon. Overleaf: Ford's famous 4–AT Tri-motor, best known as the 'Tin Goose'.

Although they had started earlier than the Americans in establishing civil airlines, the European nations were quick to discover they could not survive by passengers alone. They, too, needed the daily bread of airmail to provide the all-essential finance until the time came when passenger services could be self supporting. Most needed a great deal of money to buy new, purpose built aircraft for the day had long gone when they could cram literally a couple of passengers into the fuselage of a converted wartime aircraft. They needed money, too, for the development of airports which could handle outward and inward bound passengers with speed and efficiency. The household steps for passengers to board the aircraft, the leather flying clothing, goggles and hot water bottles for their comfort, all needed to be improved on if passengers were to be induced to fly regularly, rather than embark on a one-off flight of daring with which they could gain a high degree of one-upmanship over their friends and acquaintances. Money was needed for new buildings, control rooms, safety equipment, communications and meteorological services. No wonder that airlines did their utmost to provide adequate capacity for revenue earning mail. After all, sacks of mail could not mind being cold, or being squeezed into odd corners of an aircraft's cabin, and once contracted it was certain and regular business.

A significant aeroplane for Imperial Airways was the de Havilland D.H.66 Hercules which entered service in 1926 and was used for many pioneering services. The important factor was that it carried only seven passengers, but within its cabin was accommodation for 13.2 m³ (465 cu ft) of mail. It was a big, three engined biplane, with a multiplicity of struts and bracing wires that induced drag and limited performance. At much the same time Ford in America, Fokker in the Netherlands and Junkers in Germany were building three engined transports with a difference—all were cantilever wing monopolanes, providing new standards of reliability and performance. All were to achieve lasting fame for pioneering flights, and examples of the Junkers and Ford tri-motors were still flying in 1977, more than fifty years after the first flights of the prototypes.

Despite this change to monoplane configuration and all metal construction, manufacturers in Britain were still building big biplane airliners, such as the Handley Page H.P.42, which Anthony Fokker once described as having its own built-in headwinds. But despite this description, the 24-seat E and 38-seat W

27

versions of this airliner offered completely new standards of comfort and safety, carrying more passengers between London and Europe in the 1930s than did all other airlines combined. They are remembered with nostalgia to this day by many passengers who flew in them. They broke new ground in another way: they introduced cockpits for the flight crew. This was not generally regarded as a good thing by many passengers who seemed to think the pilot might suffer from loss of vision, or that the confines of a cabin might send him off to sleep. If they had experienced the 'joys' of an open cockpit on a winter's day, spiced by a cocktail of sleet and hail, they might have felt differently and might have realized that improved conditions could only enhance an aircrew's efficiency. But there were many changes in the offing.

On 8 February 1933 a most important aeroplane took to the air for the first time. Built by the Boeing Company in America, it had their Model number 247, and is regarded generally as one of the most significant transport aircraft ever built. It was of all metal construction in a low wing monoplane configuration, and introduced such features as retractable landing gear (to reduce drag when airborne), variable pitch propellers (to provide optimum performance for takeoff and cruising flight), control surface trim tabs (to reduce the load on aircraft controls), deicing equipment (to remove performance reducing accretions of ice that form on aerodynamic surfaces or choke the air intakes of the engines), and an automatic pilot which could relieve the flight crew from handling the flight controls over long stages once the aircraft's heading and altitude had been set. It could accommodate a crew of three and ten passengers, and its two 410 kW (550 hp) Pratt & Whitney engines and aerodynamic efficiency made it the first twin engined monoplane airliner able to climb with a full load on the power of only one engine. When introduced into service with United Air Lines (UAL) in America, the Model 247 sparked off a flurry of development in civil transport from which the nation never looked back. UAL's 247s made it possible, for the first time, for a passenger to travel coast to coast across the American continent in less than 20 hours.

Competing airlines, and in particular Transcontinental and Western Air (TWA), were soon losing valuable revenue to this 'high speed' service and needed to obtain similar—or better—aircraft. When approached by TWA the Douglas Aircraft Company produced the prototype of an improved transport within months, and the production DC–2 was not only more comfortable, carried four more passengers, and introduced wing trailing-edge flaps that improved takeoff and landing performance, but it also proved to be faster. So fast, indeed, that to the surprise of everyone a DC–2 owned by the Dutch airline KLM took second place in the 1934 MacRobertson air race from

England to Australia, flown to mark the centenary of the state of Victoria.

From the DC–2 was evolved a wider fuselage sleeper version, designated DST (Douglas Sleeper Transport), and a day version of the same aircraft, accommodating 21 passengers and designated DC–3, has by virtue of its superb capabilities and longevity earned itself the reputation of being one of the most outstanding aircraft of all time. Some 10,000 were built for service in World War 2 alone, and many examples remain in worldwide use today. The superb DC–3 swept all before it, and by the time that the Japanese struck at Pearl Harbor in 1941, 80 per cent of all scheduled airliners in the USA were DC–3s. During a twelve month period (1939–40), the airlines of America operating DC–3 services were able to report a 100 per cent safety record.

The solid foundation of routes created by the US Air Mail Service, and the provision of superb new monoplane airliners, established a strong and enduring civil aviation industry in America. The day had dawned when America, and the European nations, could begin to consider how to provide intercontinental, rather than transcontinental, services. From the earliest days of practical powered flight it had seemed logical that intercontinental air services could be most suitably provided by aircraft which could operate from and to water surfaces. Frenchman Jacques Schneider had such ideas in mind when, in 1912, he had offered a trophy for competition between waterborne aircraft, believing that this would develop a new range of airborne vessels that would speed passengers and goods over the face of the globe. When this dream became reality, as we shall see later, it was landplanes and not flying boats that ruled the seas.

There was a period in aviation history, however, when it seemed that the advocates of flying boats would be proved to be correct in their beliefs. No sooner had Britain's Imperial Airways, in conjunction with Australia's QANTAS (Queensland and Northern Territory Aerial Services), completed the air routes from London to Australia and New Zealand when, in late 1934, the British Government introduced the Empire Air Mail Scheme. This meant that in future mail for Commonwealth countries served by Imperial Airways would travel by air, and to make this possible the airline ordered from Short Brothers a fleet of four engined flying boats. The first of these S.23s, *Canopus*, made its first revenue flight on 30 October 1936. In the following year *Canopus* provided the first through service between Southampton and Durban, South Africa, and by mid-1938 Im-

perial's S.23 'Empire Boats' were operating a through service from Southampton to Sydney. They are remembered to this day for reliability, comfort, and a picturesque mode of travel now gone forever.

France reached out across the South Atlantic, its early services to South America combining both ships and waterborne aircraft. Germany, which had no colonial possessions to link by air, was able to concentrate on the creation of air routes which would prove to be sound economic propositions. But even they could not avoid the lure of the big flying boat, and in 1929 Dornier flew its giant Do X, then the largest aircraft ever built, spanning 47.9 m (157 ft), and powered by 12 engines. The original engines were subsequently replaced by 12 447 kW (600 hp) Curtiss Conquerors, but even the provision of an additional 894 kW (1200 hp) in total was inadequate. A single North Atlantic crossing that, for one reason and another took almost nine months, proved the shortcomings of the Do X, which disappeared from the aviation scene.

America, in the form of Pan American Airways, was busy considering the implications of an air service that would link America and the Philippines. To span the vast reaches of the Pacific Ocean they ordered two different flying boats, the Martin M.130 and the Sikorsky S–42. On 22 November 1935 the M.130 *China Clipper* inaugurated the airline's first mail flight across the central Pacific, but it was almost 12 months later before passengers were carried via Honolulu, Midway, Wake and Guam to Manila.

It may seem strange that there has, so far, been no

Above: A second generation turboprop powered transport, the Vickers Vanguard. Above right: A flying boat surviving in the jet age, a Dornier Do 24T–3 of Spain's sea–air rescue service. Right: A Lockheed Super Constellation piston-engined airliner.

mention of a North Atlantic service, particularly when it is recalled that the first long range ocean crossing was the transatlantic flight of Alcock and Brown in 1919. The North Atlantic route was potentially—and has since proved to be—one of the most important in the world, creating a fast link between Europe and North America. Although this had long been appreciated, it was one of the most difficult air routes to conquer, with adverse winds, unreliable weather and severe navigational problems. Conquest of the South Atlantic was much easier because far more reliable weather and comparatively straightforward navigation made it possible to fly by night or by day. Even over this route limited range was a problem not easy to resolve, for there was little point in creating an air link which needed almost all of the payload for fuel.

Germany had experimented on the South Atlantic route with a depot ship technique, and believed it could solve the North Atlantic problem by providing one or more ocean refuelling points for a seaplane which would land, be hoisted aboard, refuelled and then relaunched by catapult. Some 14 crossings were achieved by this technique, but clearly it was not suitable for a full blooded passenger service. Neither was the Short-Mayo composite with which Britain experimented, a Short S.23 flying boat carrying into the air and then launching into flight a seaplane so heavily

loaded with fuel that it could not become airborne under its own power. Imperial Airways experimented also with flight refuelling as a means of providing the necessary range. They had a flying boat carrying passengers and mail, but little fuel, and taking off in the normal manner. Once airborne it made rendezvous with a flying tanker which transferred sufficient fuel to make the transatlantic crossing practical. All of these ideas made possible a number of crossings, but they did not constitute an acceptable solution. Clearly, the requirement was an aircraft with adequate payload and range to permit the carriage of sufficient fuel and an economic load of passengers, mail or cargo.

Then, on 10 August 1938, a Lufthansa Focke-Wulf Fw 200 Condor made a non-stop crossing from Berlin to New York in just under 25 hours. The return flight, three days later, took five hours less, and these experimental flights continued until the approach of World War 2 gave rise to different priorities in aircraft construction in Germany. Twelve months before the first Condor crossing, Imperial Airways and Pan American Airways had initiated survey flights across the North Atlantic, but new-generation flying boats were needed before regular passenger/mail services could become reality. It was the American airline which inaugurated a North Atlantic passenger service on 8 July, and by then Britain was involved in military aviation matters.

War in the air 1939-1945

When the air raid sirens sounded in Britain on its first day of World War 2, on 3 September 1939, few people could have realized that almost six years would pass before the world would be at peace again. In that period of time completely new weapons would evolve, revolutionary new power plants would emerge that would change the face of postwar aviation, and a whole new science of electronics would be born. Many people were surprised that within a few moments of the siren's first wail there had been no shower of bombs from the skies. The experiences of the Spanish Civil War, vividly portrayed by the newsreels shown in cinemas around the world, had left few illusions that civilians would not become involved in the war, and almost on a front line basis at that.

On 1 September, Germany had invaded Poland, using the *Blitzkrieg* technique. Armoured columns spearheaded the attack, with close support from dive bombers which cleared pockets of enemy resistance. Fighter aircraft protected the dive bombers and conventional troops followed to consolidate the advance. It worked superbly in Poland, a nation which had a small and obsolescent air force which could not knock the German aircraft out of the sky. If courage alone was enough to win battles the Poles might have turned back the invaders. As it was the nation survived for just 17 days, leaving the Germans free to prepare themselves for a similar invasion to the west of their homeland.

On the face of it the invasion of France seemed a far more difficult task, for not only had that nation a modern air force, with such superb fighter aircraft as the Dewoitine D.520 entering its squadrons, but it had the support of Britain's Royal Air Force which the media of the day claimed was equipped with fighter aircraft that were second to none. Germany began its attack against the west, on 3 April 1940, by first over-running Denmark and Norway. When the turn of the Low Countries and France came, on 10 May, it soon became apparent that all was not quite as people had been led to believe. The much vaunted Maginot line, France's bastion against German invasion, served as little more than a landmark for the

aircraft of the *Luftwaffe* that flew overhead. France could muster between 500 and 600 fighter aircraft, most of which were obsolescent; the D.520s that were expected to shoot the German from the skies numbered about 40 of the above total. Between them, Belgium, Britain and Holland had about 60 first line fighters that could meet the *Luftwaffe* on equal terms, of which 40 were RAF Hawker Hurricanes. As land and air forces were pushed further and further westward, it was painfully clear that the approximately 1000 modern aircraft available to the *Luftwaffe* were more than capable of coping with some 500 obsolescent fighters, and the Battle of France was over almost before it had begun.

By early June 1940 only the English Channel separated the might of Germany from Britain. At that time the RAF could have called upon about 330 Hurricanes and Spitfires, plus just over 100 other fighters for the nation's defences. Fortunately, by mid-August when Germany launched her *Luftwaffe* against Britain under the code name *Adlerangriff* (Eagle Attack), production efforts by the British aircraft industry had provided a total of about 700 front line fighters, mostly Hurricanes and Spitfires, with some 300 aircraft in reserve.

Soon the skies above Britain were scrawled with contrails (condensation trails) of attacking and defending aircraft, locked in mortal combat, as the *Luftwaffe* did its utmost to vanquish the RAF. Although the Germans had superiority in numbers, it should be remembered that the RAF had the benefit of fighting a defensive battle over home ground, which meant that many damaged aircraft and slightly injured pilots survived to fight another day. In addition, the availability of radar and a fighter control system eliminated the need to fly standing patrols. Instead, a suitable force could be directed to meet each new enemy attack.

Not surprisingly, and for good psychological reasons, British victories over the invading aircraft of the *Luftwaffe* were somewhat exaggerated. In the final analysis, from both sides, records showed that the Germans had lost a total of 1244 aircraft in what has become recorded in history as the Battle of Britain.

The Royal Air Force had lost 721 aircraft, but in so doing had denied the *Luftwaffe* daylight access to the skies over Britain. Perhaps more significantly, as would become apparent in later stages of the war, many of the *Luftwaffe*'s best pilots had been killed or taken prisoner.

Unfortunately, space will not allow a detailed description of the fighter aircraft scene on a worldwide basis as it developed throughout the war. It is possible, however, to discuss the trends and innovations of the combatant nations.

As we have seen, Britain entered the war with a comparatively small number of modern low wing monoplane fighters, comprising Hurricanes and Spitfires armed with eight machine guns. Many biplane aircraft were still in service, but of these only the Gloster Gladiator remained in front line service as a fighter. The Spitfire, in steadily improving variants, was to remain in service throughout the war, but Hawker followed the Hurricane with the Typhoon and Tempest. The most significant fighter produced by the Bristol Company was the Beaufighter, which had early success as a night fighter and was developed subsequently for a wide range of combat duties. From the de Havilland company came the Mosquito, built originally as a high-speed unarmed bomber, but which earned an enviable reputation in the night fighter role. Westland, famous for its army cooperation Lysander, produced the twin engined Whirlwind fighter which had some similarity to the Mosquito.

The German aircraft industry had produced the Messerschmitt Bf 109 which was the major first line fighter in use at the beginning of the war. It, like the Spitfire, was a classic fighter aircraft which remained in service until the end of the war. Focke-Wulf evolved another superb fighter in the Fw 190, of which more than 20,000 examples were built. It differed in one major respect from the other leading fighter aircraft which have been mentioned so far—instead of an in-line liquid-cooled engine, the Fw 190 had a radial air-cooled power plant. This was of particular interest because prewar engineers had argued that for high speed combat aircraft there was no escape from the narrow-profile in-line engine which lent itself to the design of sleek, streamlined aircraft. The increased weight of the liquid cooling system and its vulnerability in combat had always been considered as disadvantages that were outweighed by the benefits of the narrow profile. While radial air-cooled engines had been developed to advanced degrees of reliability, had a better power/weight ratio than the in-line engine, and did not suffer by having an easily-damaged liquid-cooling system, it was accepted generally that if they were suitably cowled to reduce drag to a minimum they suffered from overheating problems. If cowled to provide adequate cooling, then the drag from the power unit was unacceptably high. Focke-Wulf and BMW proved the 'experts' wrong by providing a neat cowl installation of minimum diameter, with a duct which carried air to an engine cooling fan.

The closest ally of the *Luftwaffe*, Italy's *Regia*

Below: The 'Stringbag', Fairey Aviation's wonderful Swordfish carrier-based torpedo/spotter/reconnaissance biplane, renowned in Fleet Air Arm history.

Vickers Supermarine Spitfire I

SPECIFICATION

Type	single-seat interceptor fighter
Engine	Rolls-Royce Merlin III 12-cylinder Vee liquid-cooled inline, 1030 hp at take-off
Armament	eight .303-inch Browning machine guns with 300 rounds per gun
Speed	362 mph at 19,000 feet
Initial climb rate	2500 feet per minute
Climb	9 minutes 24 seconds to 20,000 feet
Ceiling	31,900 feet
Range	395 miles
Weight	4810 pounds (empty) 6200 pounds (loaded)
Span	32 feet 10 inches
Length	29 feet 11 inches
Height	12 feet 3 inches

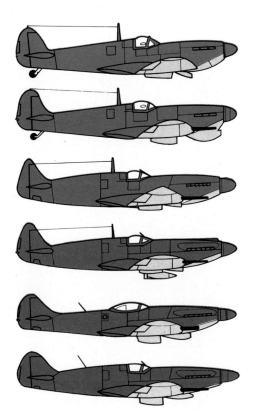

Spitfire IIA improved engine giving improved climb and ceiling; 170 Mk IIs completed as IIBs with two 20-mm cannon and four .303-inch machine guns.

Spitfire VC introduced in March 1941 with more powerful engine giving better performance; could carry bombs and was used as a fighter-bomber.

Spitfire VII extended wings for high altitude work and two-stage Merlin to give a speed of over 400 mph at 25,000 feet; ceiling 43,000 feet.

Spitfire XII first Griffon-engined model; fighter-bomber that could climb to 20,000 feet in 6 minutes 42 seconds; ceiling 40,000 feet; introduced spring 1943.

Spitfire XIVE cut-down fuselage and all-round vision bubble canopy; speed 448 mph, range 850 miles and ceiling 44,500 feet; introduced January 1944.

Spitfire XXI introduced February 1944; features stronger wing; speed 454 mph, armament four 20-mm cannon and up to 1000 pounds of bombs.

The Supermarine Spitfire, perhaps the most famous aircraft ever built, was produced in greater numbers than any other British aircraft, and was the only aircraft to remain in production throughout World War 2 in Great Britain. Developed by R.J. Mitchell from his series of floatplane racers, the first Spitfire, K/5054, flew on 5 March 1936, and was an immediate success. Deliveries to the RAF began in 1938, and by the time production ended, 20,334 Spitfires and 2408 Seafires, the naval version, had been built in 26 major marks. In that time speeds had been improved by nearly 100 mph, ceiling to 44,000 feet, range to nearly 1000 miles, and armament to two or four 20-mm cannon, two or four machine guns and 1000 pounds of bombs. The most numerous model was the Mk V, of which 6479 were built, followed by the Mk IX (5665), Mk VIII (1658), Mk I (1566) and Mk XVI (1054); 1220 examples of the Seafire Mk III were built. Originally designed for the superlative Merlin engine, the Spitfire from the Mk XII (excepting the PR XIII and Mk XVI) onwards was powered by the Rolls-Royce Griffon, a higher-powered development of the Merlin. Chief of the Spitfire's many virtues was its superb handling characteristics: its excellent manoeuvrability, good climb, fair turn of speed and adequate visibility, all combined to make it a good fighter and later fighter-bomber. Its main disadvantage was its heavy aileron control, especially at high speed.

The Supermarine Spitfire I illustrated was a machine of No 19 Squadron, RAF Fighter Command, operating from Duxford in Cambridgeshire. QV were the unit code letters of 19 Squadron from the beginning to the end of World War 2. The first service Spitfires were allocated to this squadron in 1938, when its code was WZ.

Aeronautica, had in service at the time of their entry into the war in 1940 rather more than 100 examples of a fairly successful fighter, the Fiat G.50. This, too, was powered by a radial engine, but this was because the Italian aero engine industry had been directed to concentrate on the development of radial engines. This must have seemed more than a little ironic because, as a result of Italian participation in the Schneider Trophy Contests, both Fiat and Isotta-Fraschini had developed high-powered in-line engines. An experimental G.50 powered by a Daimler-Benz in-line engine was so promising that it was decided to develop a new version, designated G.55, and powered by a 1100 kW (1475 hp) Daimler-Benz engine. This promised to be a superb fighter, but only a small number had reached squadron service when Marshal Badoglio surrendered in September 1943.

Macchi's celebrated designer, Dr Mario Castoldi, developed the C.200 Saetta fighter which remained in production throughout the war, as well as the superior C.202 Folgore which was powered by a licence built version of the Daimler-Benz in-line engine. The Folgore saw action over Malta, in Libya and Russia, and about 1500 were built before production terminated in favour of the C.250V Veltro. This was, basically, a C.202 airframe with a 1000 kW (1475 hp) Daimler-Benz engine. A high performance fighter, it was developed too late to see any significant service. The remaining fighters produced by Italy came from Reggiane SA, a subsidiary of the Caproni company. These were all of that company's 2000 Series, the most potent of which was the Re.2005 Sagitarrio which, like Macchi's C.250V, entered service too late to make any significant contribution.

Above left: Supermarine Spitfires and (below left) Sydney Camm's Hawker Hurricane, which fought off the 'Luftwaffe' in the Battle of Britain. Below: German Junkers Ju 87 Stuka dive bombers.

Among the most famous of the American fighter aircraft, one must mention the Curtiss P–40 of which nearly 14,000 examples were built to serve with the USAAF and its Allies. One of America's two twin boom fighters, Northrop's P–61 Black Widow, was designed especially for the night fighter role, and saw service with most USAAF night fighter squadrons. The other twin boom fighter was Lockheed's P–38 Lightning, a robust twin engined fighter with long range capability. Not only of great importance in the southwest Pacific, it was to prove an important escort fighter for USAAF 8th Air Force B–17 and B–24 bombers making deep penetration daylight raids over Europe. In this task, it was aided also by the single radial-engined P–47 Thunderbolt, as well as by America's best fighter of World War 2, the North American P–51 Mustang. Employed in the European theatre, their initial performance was disappointing. An experimental installation of a Rolls-Royce Merlin engine led to quantity production with Packard built Merlins installed. The combination of speed, manoeuvrability and range which resulted made the P–51 one of the most valuable fighters in Europe during the last two years of the war.

Russia, which had been invaded by Germany on 22 June 1941, produced under almost unbelievable difficulties a series of Yakovlev fighters which must also rank among the classic aircraft of World War 2. This nation was to receive also large numbers of fighter aircraft from both America and Britain, enabling its industry to concentrate upon production of other aeroplane types. There is space, to record briefly, production in Japan of the Mitsubishi A6M Zero-Sen, a carrier-based naval fighter of which almost 11,000 were built. And from Germany, with its back against the wall in 1944, came the revolutionary rocket powered Me 163, and the Me 262, the world's first turbojet fighter, which are described later.

Above: Lockheed P–38 Lightning fighters.

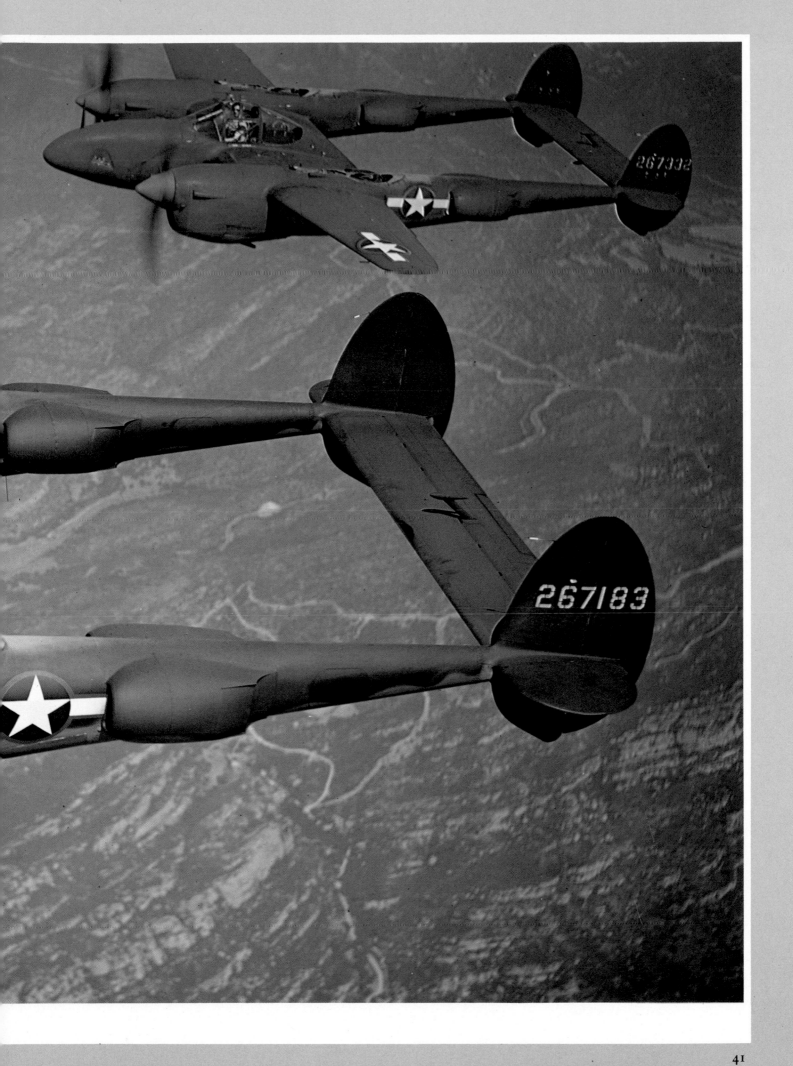

The Focke-Wulf F2 190 fighter and fighter-bomber was Germany's best such aircraft of World War 2, the other contender for this position being the Messerschmitt Bf 109. The latter, however, was an older design and reached the end of its development potential before the end of the war, unlike the Fw 190. The Focke-Wulf design was intended as a back-up in the event of the failure of the Messerschmitt fighter, and the first prototype flew on 1 July 1939. Despite initial reservations about its air cooled radial engine, the design soon showed itself to be an excellent one and the type was ordered into service.

The aircraft illustrated is a Focke-Wulf Fw 190–3 of 8/JG2 'Richthofen', that is an aircraft of the 8th *Staffel* or squadron, which was part of the 3rd *Gruppe* or wing, which was in turn part of the *Luftwaffe's* 2nd *Jagdgeschwader* (JG) or fighter group, named 'Richthofen' in honour of the great World War I ace. The vertical bar on the rear fuselage marked all III *Gruppe* aircraft, and red was the colour for the 2nd, 5th and 8th *Staffeln*. *Staffeln* 1–3 belonged to I *Gruppe*, 4–6 to II, and 7–9 to III.

Focke-Wulf Fw 190A-3

SPECIFICATIONS

Type	single-seat interceptor fighter
Engine	BMW 801Dg 14-cylinder aircooled radial, 1700 hp at take-off
Armament	two 7.92-mm MG17 machine guns with 1000 rounds per gun, two 2-cm MG151 cannon with 200 rounds per gun, and two 2-cm MGFF cannon with 55 rounds per gun
Speed	391 mph at 20,600 feet
Initial climb rate	2830 feet per minute
Climb	12 minutes to 26,250 feet
Ceiling	34,775 feet
Range	497 miles
Weight	6393 pounds (empty) 8700 pounds (loaded)
Span	34 feet 5½ inches
Length	28 feet 10½ inches
Height	12 feet 11½ inches

OPPOSITE

FW 190A-3: major early production model with extra pair of fast-firing 2-cm cannon in the wing roots, and slower-firing guns moved outboard.

FW 190D-9: first major 'long-nose' production model, introduced late in 1943; 426 mph; armament reduced to two cannon and two machine guns.

FW 190F-8: most important close-support model; it carries 24 5-cm air-to-air missiles, or 14 anti-tank missiles, or various bomb loads.

The Fw 190 was introduced into active service slowly, and was not met in combat until August 1941. However, its debut was startling, and the new radial-engined fighter quickly showed itself to be superior to any British aircraft in service. The next major series to follow the A mark was the 190-D, in 1943. This was in fact a radically redesigned version, an inline Junkers Jumo engine replacing the radial BMW 801. The new engine was cowled in the same type of nose as the earlier model, the radiator forming the annular nose of the aircraft; but the Jumo was a longer engine, and thus the fuselage had to be extended. The 'long-nose' D series was eventually developed in the highly-successful Ta 152. Armament of the D series included a 3-cm cannon in the nose. After the D came the F, a development of the A series with additional armour and reduced armament to fulfil the ground-attack role. The G series of fighter-bombers could carry up to 2,200 pounds of bombs.

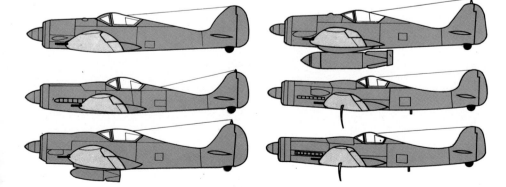

FW 190G–1: fighter-bomber; bomb-load up to 3970 pounds; preceded the F series into service; specially strengthened undercarriage for increased loads.

TA 152C–1: interceptor fighter; one 3-cm and four 2-cm cannon; 466 mph with methanol-water (MW 50) fuel injection to Daimler-Benz 603LA.

TA 152H–1: high-altitude interceptor; span 47 feet 6¾ inches; only two 2-cm cannon; speed 472 mph with nitrous-oxide injection; ceiling 48,560 feet.

The Ilyushin Il–2 was the Red Air Force's most successful and most celebrated aircraft of World War 2. In all, some 35,000 examples of the type were built, making it the most widely produced aircraft of all time. To the world in general the Il–2 is known as the *Shturmovik*, but to the combatants of the Eastern Front it was known differently: *Ilyusha* to the Russians, and *Schwarz Tod* (Black Death) to the Germans.

The task envisaged in the 1930s for the Red Air Force in any future war was that of tactical support for the army, hence the need for a fast, rugged, self-sufficient ground-attack aircraft capable of dealing knock-out blows to enemy tanks, pillboxes and infantry. Several designers produced unsuccessful prototypes, and then in late 1939 Sergei V. Ilyushin completed his CKB–57. The type proved successful after it was given a more powerful engine (1680-hp AM–38) in place of the original 1370-hp AM–35, and it was ordered into production as the Il–2 in March 1941. The most notable features of the Il–2 were the raised cockpit enclosure for the pilot and the armoured 'bath' which formed the front part of the fuselage. This was made of armour plate between 5 and 12 mm thick, and protected the engine and cockpit: examination of shot-down *Shturmoviki* usually revealed that this armour bath was intact although the rest of the machine might have been almost totally destroyed.

This first production proved moderately successful in combat, but certain defects were soon brought to the notice of the designers by combat pilots. Chief amongst these were the lack of a second crew member, a gunner, to provide rear defence, and lack of adequate armament to deal with the newer German armoured vehicles. The new requirements were finalized in spring 1942, and soon the Il–2m3 (model 3) appeared. This had a lengthened cockpit enclosure (with the armour bath lengthened also to protect it) to accommodate the rear gunner, and 23-mm VJa cannon in place of the earlier 20-mm Shvak weapons,

the muzzle velocity of which had been found to be too low.

In 1943 the VJa cannon were in turn replaced by 37-mm N–37 (or 11–P–37) cannon, which had far superior armour-piercing capabilities. So armed, the aircraft now became the Il–2m3 (Modified), entering service just in time to render invaluable service against German armour in the Battle of Kursk in July 1943. By this time the Russians were also using 132-mm rockets to replace the earlier 82-mm weapons for attacks on fixed emplacements. These large rockets could carry a hollow-charge warhead that proved absolutely devastating. Other modifications allowed the Il–2 to carry a 21-inch torpedo below the fuselage or a reconnaissance camera in the fuselage behind the gunner. The final development of the basic design was in fact a considerable redesign, and appeared too late to see service in World War 2. It was produced as the Il–10.

The Il–2 was at its most effective at low altitude, and many missions were flown at heights of below 200 feet. This meant that Il–2 pilots were often able to obtain complete surprise and attack German armour and emplacements with horizontal fire, very close to right angles with the armour plate—the most effective angle. The best tactic employed by Il–2 pilots was the so-called 'circle of death', in which the aircraft crossed the front to one side of the target and then attacked from the rear, then circled round again, allowing the aircraft behind it in the circle to launch its attack. A dozen aircraft could keep up this tactic of continuous attack for about 30 minutes until all their ammunition was expended. At Kursk 20 minutes of this tactic cost the 9th Panzer Division 70 tanks; another spell of 120 minutes reduced the 3rd Panzer Division by 270 tanks and a further attack lasting 240 minutes destroyed 240 tanks out of the 17th Panzer Division's total of 300. Undoubtedly the Ilyushin Il–2 was a magnificent fighting aircraft. It was also the Red Air Force's safest combat type of World War 2.

The Ilyushin Il–2m3 illustrated was a machine of the Assault
Regiment of the 1st Polish Mixed Air Division in 1945.

Ilyushin Il-2m3

SPECIFICATIONS

Type	two-seat ground-attack aircraft
Engine	Mikulin AM–38F 12-cylinder Vee liquid-cooled inline, 1770 hp at takeoff
Armament	two 23-mm VJa cannon, two 7.62-mm Shkas machine guns, and one 12.7-mm BS machine gun, plus one DAG 10 grenade launcher and eight 82-mm RS 82 or 132-mm RS 132 rockets, or 1325 pounds of bombs
Speed	251 mph at 6560 feet
Ceiling	19,500 feet
Range	372 miles
Weight	9604 pounds (empty) 12,136 pounds (loaded)
Span	48 feet 0½ inch
Length	38 feet 0½ inch
Height	11 feet 1½ inches

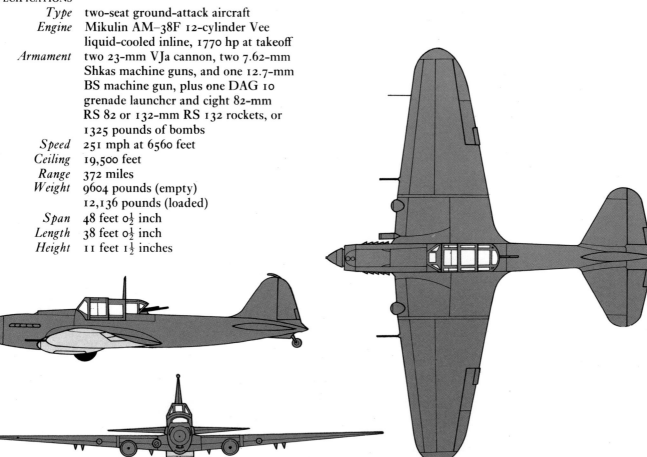

Bombers and military transports

As mentioned at the beginning of the chapter dealing with fighter aircraft, the original military use envisaged for aircraft was in a reconnaissance role. Their capability in this respect was soon found to be so important that means of shooting them out of the sky was developed as quickly as possible, and it did not take long to realize there was another method by which they could be prevented from carrying out their task: destroy them on the ground, or their supplies, or their base. This led to the original requirement for bomber aircraft. It was not long, however, before the value of the bomber was appreciated for a wide variety of military tasks so that, very soon, it was developed as a specific category of military weapon.

The potential had been realized by America's Glenn Curtiss as early as 1910, when he attacked from the air the shape of a battleship marked out by buoys on Lake Keuka. At the beginning of 1911 small explosive bombs were dropped from a US Army Wright biplane at San Francisco; and if recorded history can be considered accurate the first bombs dropped upon a capital city from an aeroplane fell upon Paris on 30 August 1914.

There was at least one man who had considered seriously the potential of a bomber aircraft, however, and this was the Russian Igor Sikorsky. In 1913 he had flown in Russia the world's first four engined aircraft. A new version named *Il'ya Muromets* was flown late the same year, and developed into a bomber aircraft in 1914. A total of about 80 were built, approximately half serving with the 'Squadron of Flying Ships', and carrying their bombs to German targets. Despite their huge size, with a wing span that averaged 30.5 m (100 ft) and a maximum speed of about 121 km/h (75 mph), it is believed that only one was destroyed by enemy fighters.

These Sikorsky IMs were, however, exceptional and it was the French who carried out the first planned bombing attacks of the war in frail looking Voisin III biplanes. Their maximum bomb load was about 59 kg (130 lb), comprising a number of small bombs which were carried on the floor of the cockpit, armed and dropped by hand by the observer. The Italians

developed and deployed the first true bomber aircraft of World War 1. The Caproni Company had evolved a large three engined aircraft, the Ca 30, before the war began, and with a requirement for a bomber they developed an improved version, designated Ca 32. A total of 164 of these aircraft were built to initiate the Italian Air Force's first bomber units, as well as its first night bomber squadron. Among other Caproni bombers which were developed during the war was the giant Ca 42 triplane, which spanned 29.9 m (98 ft 1 in) and which could carry up to 1775 kg (3913 lb) of small bombs.

As has been mentioned already, Germany sought to destroy the will of the British people to continue the war by its Zeppelin raids against England. In due course these giant airships were mastered by fighter aircraft, and Germany then turned to big twin engined Gothas to carry on the attacks. Daylight raids on London, which began in June 1917, caused a degree of alarm that was quite out of proportion to the

Right: Doyen of the German 'giant' bombers was the Zeppelin Staaken R VI, the largest aeroplane of World War I, which served with Riesenflugzeugabteilungen (Giant aeroplane squadrons) 500 & 501 on the Western Front.

damage and casualties caused. It was simply the sight of the large aircraft cruising serenely over the capital by day, above the altitude to which attacking fighters could climb in reasonable time, that created a feeling of impotence. The resulting outcry brought stronger defence against the Gothas, and when it was seen that daylight attack could prove too costly the Germans switched to night bombing. Although the majority of the heavy bombers which the Germans sent against Britain were Gothas, built by Gothaer Waggonfabrik, mention must be made of the biggest bomber to be produced in World War 1, the Zeppelin Staaken R, and examples of the R.VI—of which 18 were built—were used in the attacks on London. Spanning 42.20 m (138 ft 5½ in), this giant aeroplane had a total of 18 wheels to support its maximum takeoff weight of 11,460 kg (25,265 lb).

Britain had been slow to get down to the serious business of constructing a worthwhile strategic bomber, although quite early in the war the Admiralty's Commodore Murray Sueter had queried whether a particular Handley Page design could be scaled up into a 'bloody paralyser' of a bomber. This was to materialize in November 1916 with the entry into squadron service of the Handley Page o/100 and of the improved o/400 at a later date. These big bombers, able to carry a maximum bomb load of 908 kg (2000 lb), were the first practical heavy night bombers to enter service with any air force. In fact the o/400 came close to being cancelled, but the outcry over the German raids on London was responsible for the dubious order for 100 being increased to 700, and of these about 400 had been delivered before the end of the war. The o/400 provided convincing proof that the concept of long range strategic bombing was valid and able to make an important contribution to the military capability of an air force adopting such a policy. It was to remain integral with the thinking of RAF staff in the period between the wars, and led to the evolution of Bomber Command.

America, which became involved in World War 1 in its closing stages, produced no original bomber aircraft to participate in the conflict. In fact, only one aircraft built in the United States was in production early enough to be used in action, and this was the de Havilland D.H.4 which had been selected for large scale production in America. Capable of deployment as a light bomber, five American Expeditionary Force bomber squadrons in Europe were equipped with the type before the signing of the Armistice.

This first major conflict in which aircraft had been involved left little doubt in the minds of all military commanders that bomber aircraft might have at least some part to play in any future action. Some thought very differently, such as Hugh Trenchard, wartime commander of the Independent Force of the RAF. This Force was the first in the world to be formed to carry out a sustained strategic bombing role, and Trenchard who had campaigned for such a force was to remember its limited success and its potential when he had the task of fashioning the postwar Royal Air Force.

In the immediate postwar years, however, there was little interest in bomber aircraft, except in converting them to fulfil civil passenger or cargo carrying roles. In the final years of the war Glenn L. Martin in America had obtained a contract to build a twin engined bomber. Designated MB–2, these big machines formed the major proportion of the US Army's bomber force in the early postwar years. It was in one of these aircraft that the Army's controversial General 'Billy' Mitchell provided proof of his profound belief in strategic air power, by bombing and sinking three ex-German warships anchored in Chesapeake Bay. This early association with the Army led to the construction by Martin of the MB–10, an all metal twin engined monoplane bomber which, when tested, in 1932, proved faster than contemporary fighters. This same experience was to occur twice in Britain between the wars, the first time with the Hawker Hart, a two seat biplane bomber powered by a single Rolls-Royce Kestrel engine, which entered service in 1930. The second occasion came in 1937 when the Bristol Blenheim superseded the Hart in squadron service and demonstrated that it could fly almost 161 km/h (100 mph) faster, as well as being able to outpace the RAF's biplane fighters.

It was as well that improved designs were becoming available to the RAF, for on the other side of the English Channel Hitler's Germany was busy preparing for a new war. Precluded from building military aircraft by the terms of the Treaty of Versailles, the nation had exerted its undoubted talents in the field of aviation by designing, building and developing a new generation of highly efficient sailplanes. When Adolf Hitler came to power the peace treaty was forgotten, and soon a clandestine air force was created, its training completed away from prying eyes at Lipetsk in Russia.

German military planners had been very impressed by American experiments in the technique of dive bombing. The emphasis on the development of dive bombers was at the expense of the only long range strategic bomber which had been planned, the Heinkel He 177. The *Luftwaffe* entered the war with three primary medium bombers: the Dornier Do 17, Heinkel He 111 and Junkers Ju 88. They had, in addition, the Junkers Ju 87 dive bomber that was so successful in the early stages of the war as the spearhead of the *Blitzkrieg* technique.

Realizing the implications for Europe of a new and powerful air force in Germany, both France and Britain became involved in huge rearmament programmes. France had the technical potential of pro-

Above: The Hawker Hart light bomber which, in the 1930 Air Exercises, proved too agile for the defending fighters to intercept it.

ducing a powerful bomber force with the experience of such companies as Amiot, Bloch, Farman and Loire et Olivier, but the newly nationalized and somewhat disorganized industry failed at the critical moment. Only one really first class bomber emerged, the LeO 451, but of a total of 390 bombers in service at the outbreak of war there were only five of the 451s.

Britain entered the war in a much better position so far as bomber aircraft were concerned, and had started in 1936 the development of a new generation of multi-engined heavy strategic bombers, these emerging during the war as the Halifax, Lancaster and Stirling. But at the war's beginning it was aircraft such as the Bristol Blenheim, Handley Page Hampden, Vickers Wellington and Armstrong Whitworth Whitley which carried first the leaflets, and then the bombs, into enemy territory.

Under the dictatorship of Benito Mussolini, Italy had developed a large air force, and following the guidelines and policies of earlier years was able to draw upon the experience of such companies as CRDA Cant, Caproni, Fiat, Piaggio and Savoia-Marchetti to develop a bomber force. Italy's brief campaign in

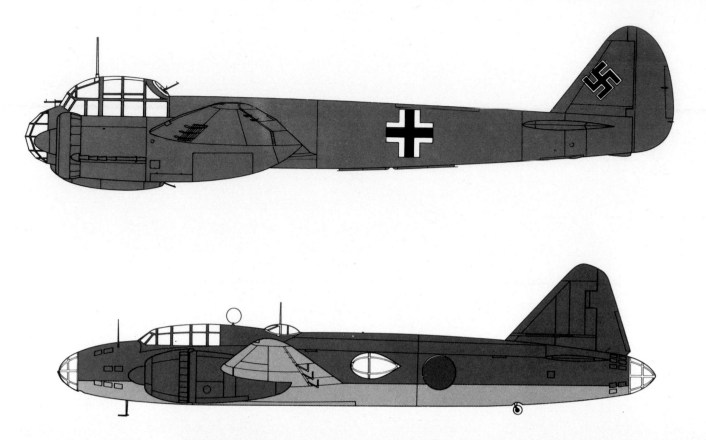

Above: Side elevation drawings of the German Junkers Ju 88 medium bomber (top), which became a maid of all work, and the Japanese Mitsubishi G4M1 'Betty' Navy Type 1 Attack Bomber. Above right: Short Stirlings, the RAF's first operational four engined monoplane bomber. Right: Boeing's B–17 Flying Fortress, the USAAC's first major strategic bomber, acquired originally as a 'defensive weapon'.

Ethiopia, and later involvement in the Spanish Civil War gave experience that was to prove valuable when the Italians entered the war in alliance with Germany.

Russia had developed some valuable medium bombers, and in particular the Ilyushin Il–4, which had a range in excess of 3200 km (2000 miles), the shorter range Tupolev Tu–2, and the long range diesel engine powered Yermolayev Yer–2. This latter aircraft had a range of more than 4800 km (3000 miles).

Japan developed a number of bombers, mostly for its Army Air Force, and with growing technological ability produced several advanced projects. One of these was the Tachikawa Ki–74, a pressurized long-range strategic bomber, an example of which set an unofficial distance record of 16,530 km (10,271 miles) in 1944. Bombers were built also by Kawasaki, Yokosuka, Nakajima and Mitsubishi, the last-mentioned being the most prolific manufacturer. Mitsubishi G3M 'Nell' and G4M 'Betty' naval bombers took part in the first attack on Pearl Harbor, and were responsible for the sinking of the battleships *Prince of Wales* and *Repulse* a few days later.

Pearl Harbor was a shattering event to the American nation and its forces determined from the first moment

Boeing B-52H Stratofortress

SPECIFICATIONS

Type	six-seat strategic heavy bomber
Engines	eight Pratt & Whitney TF-33-P-3 turbofans, 17,000 pounds static thrust each
Armament	one 20-mm ASG-21 Gatling gun, plus two AGM-28 Hound Dog winged missiles or 60,000 pounds of conventional free-fall bombs
Speed	660 mph at 20,000 feet
Climb	classified
Ceiling	55,000 feet
Range	10,000 miles
Weight	488,000 pounds (loaded)
Span	185 feet
Length	157 feet 7 inches
Height	40 feet 8 inches

Above: A Boeing B–52H eight-turbojet-powered strategic bomber, in service in late 1977 with the USAF's Strategic Air Command. Many B–52G and H Stratofortresses have been modified for a new low-level capability.

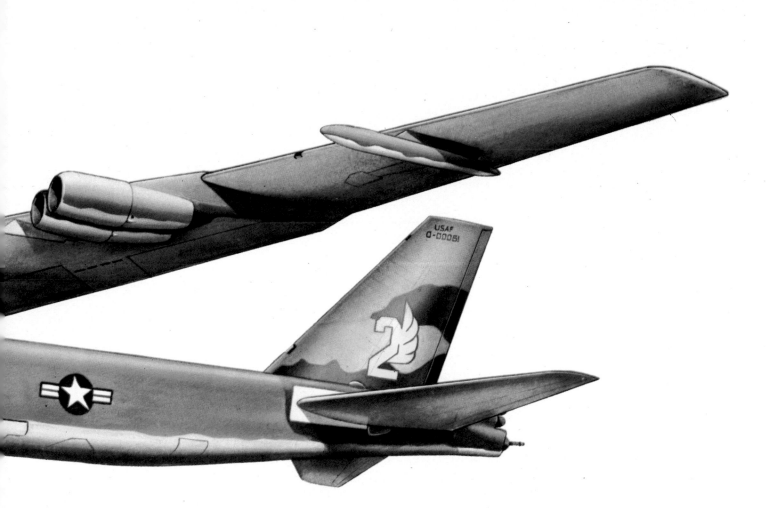

to avenge those who had died on 7 December 1941. After the all out propaganda of General Mitchell for the development of a strategic bomber force, and his subsequent disgrace and resignation from the air force, there had been an almost continuous Army versus Navy battle in which the Army had been the loser so far as the acquisition of a strategic bomber force was concerned. B–17s were finally ordered but only a handful were completed when America became involved in the war. Pearl Harbor signalled the beginning of the American aircraft industry's change-over to the production of military aircraft and soon there were growing fleets of four engined B–17 Fortresses and B–24 Liberators, as well as twin engined Douglas DB–7s, A–26 Invaders, Martin B–26 Marauders and North American B–25 Mitchells. These types were particularly valuable in the European theatre, but the vast distances of the Pacific led to the development of the Boeing B–29 Superfortress which made it possible to drop the two atomic bombs on Hiroshima and Nagasaki, speeding the surrender of Japan whose cities had been devastated by B–29 incendiary bomb attacks.

The war in the Pacific saw the development of long range aircraft, not only as bombers but also as trans-port aircraft able to provide a never ending stream of supplies and reinforcements, and to act in a casualty evacuation role on their return flight. Transports had been developed in the European theatre not only for the rapid movement of troops and supplies, but also as transport and launching vehicles for airborne para-troops. In the post World War 2 years this develop-ment of military transport aircraft has grown in importance, and the major powers now have fleets which can carry a sizeable force to almost anywhere in the world.

The development of aircraft with the capability to carry huge loads across the world was speeded by the evolution of an entirely new power plant, with initial examples of these engines being built and tested almost simultaneously in Britain and Germany. It was in 1928, while a cadet at RAF Cranwell, that Frank Whittle had published a thesis which laid down the basic thermodynamics of the new gas turbine engine, but it took another nine years before he was able to run a prototype engine. In Germany Dr Pabst von Ohain had been working quite independently, and with no knowledge of Whittle's work, to produce a similar type of engine in the same year, though at that time von Ohain's turbojet was using hydrogen fuel. In both countries aircraft were built to test these new power plants: Germany's Heinkel He 178 flew first, on 27 August 1939, and Britain's Gloster E.28/39 on 15 May 1941. Britain gained an early lead in gas

turbine technology, but very soon new and improved engines of ever increasing power were being built by several nations.

In mid-July 1944 the world's first turbojet powered bomber entered service, albeit in very small quantities. This was the German Arado Ar 234 Blitz, and from the initial operations of this 14.44 m (46 ft 3½ in)

Above: The North American XB–70 Valkyrie tail-first delta-winged Mach 3 strategic bomber. Below: Artist's impression of Rockwell International B–1A swing-wing Mach 2.2 strategic bomber for the USAF. Both this and the Valkyrie have been axed on account of their cost.

span aircraft, which demonstrated a maximum speed of 852 km/h (529 mph) at altitude, have evolved new generations of large bomber and transport aircraft. Illustrating development in this field are such machines as the American B–1 bomber which can fly at twice the speed of sound and the C–5 Galaxy transport weighing some 345 tonnes (340 tons) at takeoff. The evolution of aircraft like this has speeded the development of jet airliners which have transformed air travel into a vast operation that pioneer aviators would probably not have imagined possible.

Airliners in the jet age

As recorded earlier, America had started the first transatlantic passenger services with the big Boeing Model 314 Clippers. Throughout the war this service continued to operate, and the flying boats which had served Britain and other countries so well in the development of long range air routes did their utmost to maintain some services until the return of peace.

In the early days of aviation it had seemed logical to operate aeroplanes which could take off from and land on water, since the major portion of the Earth's surface is covered by water. (There were even some who believed that in the event of a crash landing the

Below: The de Havilland Comet 4 in BEA insignia.

water would cause less damage than a land surface!) World War 2 changed this completely, especially America's involvement in war against Japan, which necessitated the regular supply and maintenance of a vast force fighting a difficult hit and run conflict on the far side of the Pacific Ocean. This required the development of bomber and transport aircraft with considerable range capability, and for a variety of reasons it was better that these should operate from a land rather than a water surface. Thus when VJ day signalled that, after six long years, the world had returned to peace, the landplane had acquired dominance and a new status which meant that the era of the flying boat was also coming to a close. There

were, of course, factors other than range alone. To provide bases from which this new type of landplane could operate, long concrete runways had been built throughout the world and, in the main, were far more convenient for potential passengers than a sea or river base. Among the problems of bases on or beside water was the difficulty of ensuring that the takeoff and landing area was completely free from floating debris, of getting passengers from shore to boat if there were extensive shallows, and of course there were enormous numbers of locations that required an air terminal which were remote from any large mass of water.

World War 2 had brought a host of improvements that were to speed the inauguration of new services that would network the globe. And there were plenty of operators who were anxious to get started, because there was little doubt that there would be an enormous upsurge in air travel, for countless numbers of service personnel—of all services—had flown as routine in the war just ended. They knew that flying had become a convenient and fast means of travel for ordinary men and women and that, no longer, was it reserved only for supermen with iron nerves.

Some of the improvements which had made air travel so very different from the tentative services of

the 1930s included reliable and far more powerful engines (not including the new turbojets which were in their infancy and with very high fuel consumption); use of the monoplane configuration, with better streamlining and improved structures; and the introduction of electronic equipment to make possible better communications—and over very long ranges—and radar and other measuring techniques to simplify navigation to any point on the earth's surface.

The fortunes of war had favoured the American aircraft industry, for by agreement among the Allies that nation had concentrated its talents on the development and production of long range bombers and transports. The very different type of war being fought in the European theatre had required the aircraft industries of Britain, Germany and other European nations to specialize in the evolution of short/medium range aircraft. Thus, at the war's end the American industry was ready, and able, to supply the world's needs for transport aircraft—initially by the production of civil versions of existing bombers and transports. And this meant that airlines equipped

Above: Boeing's famous Model 747 'Jumbo Jet', which first introduced the wide body transport into airline service. Left: The 747 was followed by the McDonnell Douglas DC–10.

themselves with products of the Boeing, Douglas and Lockheed Companies, and have continued to buy equipment from these suppliers, giving the American aircraft industry a lead which it has maintained up to the present.

Among the direct developments from United States military aircraft was the Boeing Model 377 Stratocruiser, a four engined model derived from the B–29 Superfortress. When introduced on the North Atlantic route in 1949, the Stratocruiser set completely new standards of speed and comfort, and it is interesting to record that those operators who equipped with this aeroplane gained a market lead over their competitors which they have retained to this day. In due course America's purpose built new generation of airliners began to appear on the world's travel routes, and included such aircraft as the Lockheed Super Constellation, Douglas DC–7B and DC–7C 'Seven Seas', and in 1957 the Lockheed L.1649A Starliner. This latter aircraft represented the peak of development of the long range piston engined airliners, and not only provided its passengers with safe and comfortable travel but also offered to the airlines which operated it an aircraft with a high utilization factor and profits to match.

Postwar civil operations in Britain followed a similar pattern, with conversions or quick derivations of wartime bombers and transports filling the gap until new generation aircraft began to appear. Thus, for example, the Vickers Viking was a close cousin of the Wellington which had served the RAF so well throughout the war; and the Avro Lancaster sired such airliners as the Lancastrian, York and Tudor.

The Lancastrian was particularly interesting, emerging from a Lancaster III obtained by Trans Canada Air Lines (TCA) for conversion to civil use. With gun turrets removed and the cavities faired over, and with windows added to the rear fuselage, TCA used this machine for evaluation, and in due course this aircraft inaugurated TCA's transatlantic service on 22 July 1943. From this first functional modification a number of Lancastrians were produced, and this aircraft was Britain's first to have a true South Atlantic capability. Fortunately for Britain, there had been a fair degree of foresight within the aircraft industry before the war's end, and the Brabazon Committee of 1942/43 had worked hard to provide guidelines without the benefit of a crystal ball. Thus, not all of its recommendations, however sound in 1943, were still valid at the end of the war. The beautiful Princess flying boats created by Saunders Roe, for example, were born into a postwar world which no longer needed water borne aircraft to cater for its long distance requirements. The most important achievement of the Brabazon Committee was that it made Britain's aircraft industry think seriously about the future at a time when they would not otherwise have looked up from their production lines. And one of its recommendations was to prove vital to the continued prosperity of the industry, namely that emphasis should be placed on the development of the infant gas turbine engine, especially for civil applications.

During the war, as mentioned earlier, America had been responsible for the design and development of long range transports and, as a result, was in a particularly happy position at the war's end. Not only had the design capability and constructional know how been acquired; the industry could put into commercial service, at short notice, converted aircraft capable of intercontinental services on a worldwide basis. Its first generation of passenger airliners had every chance of being world beaters.

Britain, on the other hand, was likely to produce good short/medium range transports, but only mediocre long range civil airliners at its first generation. In either event, America would almost certainly retain the market lead it had enjoyed in the late 1930s when Douglas had supplied DC–2s and DC–3s to civil operators outside of the United States.

Britain had a considerable lead over America in gas turbine engine technology, and it made sense to the design team of the de Havilland company to put their money on this engine and to jump one generation beyond the Americans. It was a brave scheme, involving far more than designing a new airframe and using turbojets to speed it through the air. Early military experience had shown that at low altitudes the turbojet drank fuel at an alarming rate. At high altitude, however, fuel consumption fell to more acceptable levels; in addition, travel at these altitudes would provide passengers with smooth, fast travel, high above the worst of the weather which causes turbulence and bumpy conditions. Unfortunately, flight at altitudes of up to 11.3 km (7 miles) meant that passengers would have to wear oxygen masks, unless alternative means were provided to allow them to breathe normally. Thus, de Havilland's new airliner was designed with a pressurized cabin, which meant that its structure had to be able to withstand a pressure of 0.57 bars (8.25 lb/sq in). To lift this very new airframe, crew of 7 and 36 passengers to its operating height, 4 de Havilland Ghost turbojet engines were mounted cleanly within the wing roots.

Known as the Comet 1, this aircraft inaugurated the world's first regular passenger service to be flown by a turbojet powered airliner on 2 May 1952, linking London and Johannesburg in an elapsed time of 23 h 34 min. The superb and smooth performance of these aircraft, their speed and comfort by comparison with even the most advanced piston engined airliner, and their ability to operate with almost unbelievable regularity, gave convincing proof that the gamble had paid off. Britain's new turbine powered airliner appealed to both passengers and operators and the stage was set for large scale sales.

Then, tragically, there came news of two Comet losses, one in seemingly inexplicable circumstances. When a third South African Airways Comet was lost, in April 1954, the type was grounded pending a full investigation. Fragments of a BOAC Comet were recovered off the Isle of Elba, and divers of the Royal Navy recovered—in small pieces—almost 70 per cent of the aircraft. At the Royal Aircraft Establishment, Farnborough, England, scientists and engineers painstakingly sorted, identified and pieced together the torn pieces of metal, until they were able to establish that the aircraft's cabin had disintegrated as a result of metal fatigue, caused by repetitive cycles of pressurization. This news was given to aircraft manufacturers all over the world, who soon learned to build failsafe structures able to withstand these, and increasing demands in complete safety. But for Britain this information came too late; by the time that de Havilland had built their new Comet 4, America had clawed back the British lead and put into service the magnificent Boeing 707. First flown in July 1954, the 707 is in worldwide airline service in 1977, and has demonstrated reliability and structural integrity of a high order.

Relying on the same lead in turbine development, Britain held more than one ace and had, in fact, played the first of these before the Comet had entered service. This came with the Certification of the Vickers Viscount on 28 July 1950, and on the following day a Viscount recorded the world's first scheduled passenger service to be flown by a turbine powered airliner. The power plant of the Viscount differed from that selected for the Comet. Instead of relying upon the high velocity jet efflux of the turbojet to provide propulsive energy, the engines of the Viscount were turboprops, in which the gas turbine drives a propeller through the medium of a reduction gear. The resulting engine has a lower fuel consumption, while retaining the superb smoothness of a turbine, which has no reciprocating components.

The Viscount was followed by the elegant Bristol Britannia, also turboprop powered, which on 1 February 1957 became the world's first long range turboprop powered transport in service, and on 19 December of the same year inaugurated the world's first transatlantic service to be flown by a turbine powered airliner. Sales to foreign operators of both the Viscount and Britannia were, at the outset so good that it appeared that there had been a significant break into the world market. Such thoughts were premature, and if analysed not really surprising.

Above: The Airbus Industrie A300B2 Airbus, Europe's wide body transport, which is built by a consortium of five European nations and powered by US engines.

Much of an airline operator's capital is tied up in ground equipment and spares, especially if he is equipped to a standard that will enable him to provide regular and safe services with well trained ground and air crews. It is no easy matter, either practically or financially, to change horses in midstream, and if a particular manufacturer has evolved a good basic aircraft which, in the course of time, is developed and then ultimately proliferates into a number of variants suitable for differing requirements, then there is every reason to suppose that the operator will retain loyalty to that company.

To take a particular manufacturer to illustrate this point, the Boeing Company in America had, it will be remembered, introduced the first truly modern airliner—the Boeing 247—in 1933. It continued to build a succession of steadily improved aircraft, and entered the jet age in October 1958 when the four turbojet Model 707 was introduced on Pan American's North Atlantic service. It was followed by an almost identical intermediate range model 720, a short/medium range Model 727 with three turbojets, and then by a short range twin engined Model 737. There was a general similarity between all four models and a fairly high commonalty of components; it made good sense to buy Boeing products, because a large operator had aircraft with the right characteristics for a variety of routes.

The 727, with three engines, is of interest because it highlights a new trend introduced first by French Sud-Ouest, part of that country's nationalized aircraft industry. First flown in May 1955 the Caravelle, as the type was named, features two Rolls-Royce Avon turbojets mounted one on each side of the aft fuselage. This configuration was chosen because, at that time, it seemed the best way of ensuring that the aircraft's wing was aerodynamically 'clean' (uncluttered by engine mountings) and giving improved takeoff performance, as well as a much quieter cabin for its passengers. Other manufacturers followed suit, and Boeing who sought to provide more economic operation with its short/medium range 727 elected to use three engines, mounting one on each side of the aft fuselage and the third above the fuselage at the base of the fin. Douglas in America, BAC and Hawker Siddeley in Britain and Ilyushin and Tupolev in Russia have all used this layout.

The last-mentioned company, which used the rear-engined layout for its Tu–134, introduced on international services by Aeroflot in September 1967, was no newcomer to the use of turbine power. In fact, there had been something of a sensation among aircraft manufacturers in the West when, in March 1956, a Tupolev Tu–104 airliner carried Soviet officials to London Airport. Powered by two turbojets, these aircraft entered service on Aeroflot's Moscow–Irkutsk route on 15 September 1956, establishing the world's second turbine powered airline service. On this initial route the schedule was cut from twenty hours to just over seven, revolutionizing civil air travel in Russia, and by the time that Boeing's 707 was just beginning its career, Aeroflot had networked the Soviet Union with fast and comfortable air services.

So far in this chapter we have been looking primarily at the big league, but it must be remembered that there is an enormous requirement for smaller, more economic aircraft, with which to operate the domestic routes. Perhaps less glamorous than intercontinental travel, and the big gleaming airliners which speed their passengers around the world, there is a huge demand for short haul services to carry people for business or pleasure.

In this category of smaller airliners one must mention first the Fokker-VFW F27 Friendship, built in the Netherlands by the descendant company of that established by Anthony Fokker. It followed the lead of the Viscount, by using two turboprop engines to power the initial version which had accommodation for 40 passengers. Current production F27 Mk 600 aircraft have maximum accommodation for 60 passengers, and continuing production in 1977 emphasizes the excellent design of an aircraft which first flew in 1955. Civil airliners in this category proliferate around the world and it is possible to mention only a few of these. Australia is developing currently a small twin turboprop utility aircraft: known as the Nomad, its 15 passenger N24 version may well see extensive use on a national basis. Canada has had in production since 1965 a most attractive twin turboprop named the Twin Otter, of which around 500 have been sold. Seating a maximum of 20 passengers, it has been bought by many foreign operators. The Twin Otter was designed and manufactured by de Havilland Canada, and this Company—in 1977—began the introduction into service of a new 50 seat STOL (short takeoff and landing) transport known as the Dash 7. Of particular importance to people who live near airports is the fact that the Dash 7, and many new aircraft entering airline service, have been given the benefit of special attention to ensure that they make less noise than their predecessors. Beech and Cessna in America have produced some superb business/commuter aircraft. VFW-Fokker in Germany—VFW emanating from the famous Focke-Wulf and Heinkel companies—has, with financial backing from the government, developed a 40/44 seat twin engine transport known as the VFW 614; the other half of the organization, Fokker-VFW in the Netherlands, began production deliveries in 1969 of a twin turbine 55/85 seat short range transport designated F28 Fellowship. Britain's contribution to this important class of aircraft includes the BAC One-Eleven, Hawker Siddeley HS 125, and Short SD3-30.

Some of the above mentioned aircraft are powered by what are known as 'turbofan' engines, in which air is ducted past the compressor, combustion area and turbine, to provide a large volume of cold air to mix with the jet efflux from the turbine. Research had shown that the noise that used to be associated with a jet engine was caused mainly by the hot exhaust gases causing turbulence as they mixed with the atmospheric air, and that this could be reduced if the velocity of the jet efflux could be slowed in relation to the atmospheric air. The large volume of bypass air, when mixed with the jet efflux, achieves this and makes a quieter engine. It is fortunate that this development has come about, for the enormous thrust needed to lift modern generation 'Jumbo' jets into the air would otherwise be ear shattering.

And so we have come to this latest and 'greatest' creation of the world's aircraft industry, first proposed by Boeing in the mid-1960s: the wide body airliner. When the company announced that it was to build a new generation transport, with accommodation for a maximum of 500 passengers, there was an immediate prediction of disaster. And because everything connected with the airliner was large scale, it was quickly nicknamed the 'Jumbo Jet'. Boeing has expressed its dislike of the title, but like it or not this Boeing 747, the world's first wide body airliner, will almost certainly be remembered and recorded in aviation history as the Jumbo.

The 747 entered service with Pan American on its New York/London route on 22 January 1970, since when about 300 have been built. It was followed into service by the McDonnell Douglas DC-10 in August 1971, and by the Lockheed TriStar in April 1972. These big airliners have brought tremendous changes to intercontinental routes by providing regular and reliable travel with standards of comfort and service which have reduced fatigue enormously.

Europe, considering itself unable to market an airliner in the same category, formed a consortium to design, build and market a twin turbofan short/medium range transport. Introduced into service by Air France on 23 May 1974, this 220/320 seat transport is powered by General Electric turbofans which provide the Airbus, as it is called, with perhaps the best 'Community relations' noise levels of any airliner yet introduced into service.

And way back in 1962, when the Jumbo was little more than a twinkle in the eyes of Boeing's design team, Britain and France signed an agreement to build a supersonic transport (SST), and to emphasize Anglo-French collaboration it was named Concorde. Between three and four years later both America and Russia announced their intention to build SSTs, by Boeing and Tupolev respectively; the former had the designation Model 2707-300. This, unfortunately, was axed in 1971 when the US Senate declined to provide financial backing, leaving Tupolev's Tu-144

to contend against the Aérospatiale/BAC Concorde. The Tu–144 was the first to fly, on 31 December, 1968, the first French-built Concorde prototype making its maiden flight on 2 March 1969. Russia's Tu–144 was also the first into service, with regular flights between Moscow and Alma-Ata in Kazakhstan starting on 26 December 1975. These, however, carried only mail or other cargo, and it was the British Airways G–BOAA and Air France F–BVFA Concordes which began simultaneous passenger services on 21 January 1976.

Above: The Anglo/French Concorde. Top: Russia's Tupolev Tu–144 SST, sometimes dubbed Concordski in the West because of its similarity to Concorde. Both are of similar size, with accommodation for a maximum of about 140 passengers, and both are designed for a normal cruising speed of Mach 2.2. Both represent great technological achievements, but there is some doubt as to whether they are large enough to be economically viable. One intriguing question is whether a second generation SST will appear, or if development costs and energy or ecological problems will prevent their birth.

The jet fighter story

In the three preceding chapters we have seen how the gas turbine engine was evolved almost simultaneously in Britain and Germany, and have accepted the fact that these exciting new power plants were used to equip some aircraft in the closing stages of World War 2. We have seen how designers have made it possible to create a whole new range of bomber, military transport and civil transport aircraft which have changed the face of aviation.

In dealing with the development of jet fighters, high performance reconnaissance aircraft and formidable new attack aircraft, we shall have the opportunity of seeing how jet powered aeroplanes have evolved from the rather tentative machines which Britain and Germany first deployed operationally.

Of necessity, most of the development was with small research or fighter type aircraft, for the turbine engines of the first postwar years were somewhat limited in power output and, in fact, Gloster Meteor F.3s which were in service with the RAF in 1945 had a maximum speed of 668 km/h (415 mph), while the twin piston engined de Havilland Hornet flew in prototype form in July 1944 and demonstrated a maximum level speed of 780 km/h (485 mph): the piston-engine/propeller combination, at the peak of its development, was still holding its own. Clearly, the turbine engine was in its infancy, while the piston engine had matured to this high performance by a process of refinement over a period of 60 years. The potential of a gas turbine after a few years of research and improvement was likely to be enormous in terms of power/weight ratio, and it could be assumed also that in this programme of evolution it should prove possible to improve fuel consumption.

Between existing aircraft, and those which might evolve in a comparatively short space of time, there was a wide technological gap. Pilots of high speed fighter aircraft, such as the American Lockheed Lightning and British Hawker Typhoon, had discovered that sometimes, and especially in a dive, their aircraft would shudder inexplicably and frighteningly and reported the occurrence. They were the lucky ones, because in some instances the aircraft were literally shaken to pieces, with wings or tail units being torn away. This was a problem which had to be resolved before new generation jet powered aircraft could fly at the much higher speeds which would soon be possible. Research scientists working with model aircraft in high speed wind tunnels were aware that as an aerofoil surface approached the speed of sound (1223 km/h: 760 mph at sea level, falling to 1062 km/h: 660 mph above 10,970 m: 36,000 ft) the smooth flow

Left: The first jet fighter in USAF service was the Lockheed P–80, and illustrated is the T–33 trainer version. Above: The F–86 Sabre was the USAF's first swept wing jet fighter.

over the wing ceased. Instead, the air became compressed ahead of the wing leading-edge, causing violent shock waves that, clearly, had been responsible for the buffeting of their aircraft which had been reported by pilots. This, at first, seemed a barrier to very high speed flight, but German wartime research had shown that thinner section swept wings (that is with an angle of less than 90 degrees formed between the centreline of the rear fuselage and the wing leading-edge) made it possible for an aircraft to approach very near to the speed of sound before the buffeting began. Scientists in America resolved to

investigate this problem, known as 'compressibility', and the Bell Aircraft Company was contracted to build a small piloted research aircraft with a very strong structure that would be able to withstand severe buffeting without failure. And to enable it to exceed the speed of sound, the X–1, as this famous little aircraft was designated, had a powerful rocket engine. For a number of reasons it was desirable to carry out the tests at high altitude, but as the X–1's engine consumed about a ton of fuel per minute it was necessary to lift it to some 9145 m (30,000 ft) beneath a Boeing B–29 'mother-plane' before air launching the X–1 to climb away to its test height.

The pilot responsible for the early testing of the X–1 was a young officer of the USAF, Charles 'Chuck' Yeager, and each time the rocket plane was

Above: BAC F.6 Lightnings in service with the RAF. The Lightning was Britain's first truly supersonic single seat fighter.

released from the B–29 he flew it progressively nearer to the speed of sound—recorded as Mach 1—until at Mach 0.94 (94 per cent of the speed of sound) the little aircraft was buffeted so violently that there were moments when he felt the task was impossible. Then, on 14 October 1947, Yeager decided the moment had come when he must succeed or fail. Approaching the critical speed rapidly, with the rocket engine developing full power, the buffeting reached an almost unbelievable intensity and Yeager's control of the aircraft was only marginal. Suddenly, without any warning, the buffeting stopped: 'Chuck' Yeager had flown the X–1 through the invisible 'sound barrier' to become the first man in the world to fly faster than the speed of sound. Later, in the Bell X–1A, Yeager was to attain a speed of 2655 km/h (1650 mph), and the stage was set to use this new knowledge to build a very different range of combat and reconnaissance aircraft.

It is convenient to continue the story of the transition from research aircraft to practical hard hitting fighters in America, but it must be realized that the growing capability of such machines resulted from international research and development, rather than from the work of any one nation. Because of Britain's initial lead in the development of turbine engines,

the first American jet fighter—the Bell P–59 Airacomet—was powered by two General Electric turbojet engines which derived directly from the early Whittle designs. It was followed by the Lockheed P–80 Shooting Star and the prototype, powered by a British de Havilland H–1 turbojet, flew for the first time on 8 January 1944. An XP–80B version of this design set a new speed record of 1003.9 km/h (623.8 mph) in 1947, and the later F–80C (instead of P–80C because of a change in USAF designations) was built in large numbers. Many of these aircraft were involved in the Korean War, and it was in an F–80C that the USAF's Lt Russel Brown destroyed a Russian MiG–15 jet fighter, the first recorded combat victory involving an engagement of two jet powered aircraft, on 8 November 1950.

At about the same time that the Lockheed P–80 prototype made its first flight, the Republic Aviation Corporation was involved in the design of a jet powered fighter/bomber to replace the P–47 Thunderbolt in squadron service. The resulting F–84 Thunderjet was the last subsonic (below the speed of sound) fighter to enter USAF service, and because it was intended for a tactical role it required rather more range than the average fighter. Range can, of course, be increased by providing for additional internal or

Far left: The Lockheed U–2 high altitude reconnaissance aircraft, capable of flight at 21 km (13 miles) above the earth. Above left: Lockheed's F–104 Starfighter, almost a manned missile, with a wing area of only 18.22 m² (196.1 sq ft), by comparison with the 21.45 m² (231 sq ft) wing of the Spitfire 1. Below left: The Anglo/French Jaguar single seat light tactical support aircraft, in service with both the British and French air forces, has a Mach 1.5 speed capability.

external fuel, but in either event it means that fewer weapons or less ammunition can be carried. As a result it was decided to provide the F–84 with flight refuelling capability, a technique mentioned briefly in connection with early attempts to create a trans-atlantic passenger service. It entails a tanker making rendezvous with the aircraft which, generally, has taken off heavily laden with everything but fuel and, once airborne, fills its tanks from the flying tanker. This technique has become important for many types of military aircraft, including such diverse examples as supersonic fighters and decidedly subsonic heli-copters, and makes it possible for vital short range aircraft to acquire long range capability when necessary. When the Republic F–84 entered service in 1947, the prototype of North American Aviation's F–86 Sabre, the first swept wing fighter to enter service, was beginning its flight test programme, and during this it exceeded a speed of Mach 1 in a shallow dive, being the first American production aircraft to do so.

By the time that the F–86 entered service, North American's F–100, evolved from the F–86, was on the drawing board. Basically a larger version of the Sabre with a more powerful engine, it featured a low set wing with 45 degrees of sweepback. It proved to be a superb machine, the world's first operational fighter able to exceed the speed of sound in level flight. On 29 October 1953 a YF–100A prototype established at low altitude a world speed record of 1215.29 km/h (755.149 mph), and two years later the F–100C, which had a maximum level speed of Mach 1.25, set a world speed record of 1323.09 km/h (822.135 mph). The era of the supersonic combat fighter had dawned.

The Super Sabre was used extensively during the war in Vietnam, but was in due course superseded by such aircraft as the McDonnell Douglas F–4 Phantom II, with a maximum speed capability of more than Mach 2, and the 'swing-wing' General Dynamics F–111 which combined short field takeoff and landing performance with a top speed at altitude of Mach 2.5, plus a maximum range on internal fuel well in excess of 4825 km (3000 miles).

War in Korea and Vietnam brought about many changes in American military thinking. Combat air-craft capable of speeds of Mach 1.5 were not cheap to build. And when two aircraft meet in combat with a closing speed of more than 3200 km/h (2000 mph), which is rather faster than 0.8 km (0.5 miles)/second, it needs complicated and costly electronic systems to cope with the constantly changing combat situation, the aiming and firing of weapons, as well as to provide

Above: General Dynamics F–111 'swing wing' fighter with the wings in the unswept position for landing, takeoff and slow speed manoeuvre.

McDonnell Douglas F-4 Phantom II

SPECIFICATIONS (F-4B)

Type	two-seat interceptor and attack aircraft
Engines	two General Electric J79-GE-8 turbojets, 17,000 pounds thrust each with afterburning
Armament	six Raytheon Sparrow III, or 4 Sparrow III and 4 General Electric Sidewinder I air-to-air missiles, plus up to 16,000 pounds of external stores. These can be made up of a mixture of 250-, 500-, 750-, or 1000-pound bombs, nuclear weapons, rocket launchers, landmines, napalm bombs, chemical warfare bombs, leaflet bombs, and sometimes GAM-83A Bullpup missiles and 20-mm Vulpod or 7.62-mm Minipod gun packs
Speed	1548 mph at 48,000 feet (Mach 2.4)
Initial climb rate	28,000 feet per minute
Ceiling	71,000 feet
Combat radius	900 miles
Ferry range	2300 miles
Weight	28,000 pounds (empty)
	56,000 pounds (loaded)
Span	38 feet $4\frac{7}{8}$ inches
Length	58 feet $3\frac{1}{8}$ inches
Height	16 feet 3 inches

The McDonnell Douglas F-4 Phantom II can justly
be claimed to be the best combat aircraft to have served
with the air forces of the Western world since 1945. Although more
advanced types gradually began to replace the Phantom in 1975,
this versatile machine will still continue to contribute greatly to the
attack and defence capability of the West for some time to come.
The Phantom I of 1946 was the US Navy's first operational jet aircraft,
and the development of the Phantom II can be traced from its earlier
namesake via the F-2H Banshee, the F-3H Demon, and the USAF's
F-101 Voodoo. On its own initiative, McDonnell started design work on a new
carrier-borne fighter in 1953. By the end of 1954 the Navy had decided that it needed
a larger, faster type than had originally been envisaged, and McDonnell redesigned
the F-3H-G idea so that by August 1956 construction of the XF-4H-1 prototype
Phantom II could begin; it was completed in April 1958 and proved
immediately successful. Squadron service began in February 1961.

A US Navy F-4B of the VF-114 Fighter Squadron comes
in to land. Note the number of pylon-mounted stores
still carried, the arrester hook, and the drooped
leading edges and flaps.

F-4 PHANTOM II MARKS

F-4A: 23 prototypes and 24 training aircraft for US Navy.
F-4B: production ship-board fighter and attack aircraft for the US Navy and US Marine Corps.
RF-4B: unarmed reconnaissance variant for US Marine Corps.
F-4C: air superiority and close support fighter for the USAF.
RF-4C: unarmed reconnaissance variant for USAF.
F-4D: USAF fighter with improved weapons system. Also ordered by Iran.
F-4E: USAF fighter with integral cannon armament. Also ordered by Japan and Israel.
RF-4E: reconnaissance variant of F-4E. Ordered by the West German Air Force or *Luftwaffe*.
F-4G: experimental adaptation of F-4B for automatic deck-landing trials.
F-4J: Improved US Navy and Marine Corps combat type.
F-4K: Spey-engined version of F-4J for Royal Navy.
F-4M: RAF fighter-bomber/reconnaissance version of F-4K.

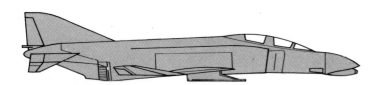

ABOVE AND LEFT Three views of the Phantom. Note the massive fuselage, 'droop snoot' nose, anhedral tailplane and dihedral only on the outer panels of the wings.

all weather capability, navigation, direction finding, communications and identification. It is not surprising that such equipment can cost more than the aircraft in which it is installed, or that an advanced modern weapon system—that is the aircraft complete with its electronics, weapons, and other specialized equipment—has been quoted as being worth more than its weight in gold.

The requirement for, and the development of, advanced military aircraft has not been confined to the needs of air forces. From the earliest days of military aviation navies have shown considerable interest in aircraft, initially to extend their 'eyes' beyond the horizon. America's General Mitchell had demonstrated that even heavily armoured battleships could be at the mercy of comparatively low performance aircraft, and the truth of this was demonstrated vividly at Pearl Harbor in December 1941 with 18 ships sunk or seriously damaged in a matter of minutes. Confirmation of the potential of the aeroplane came three days later when HMS *Prince of Wales* and *Repulse* were sunk by Japanese aircraft. War in the Pacific, in general, was to emphasize the importance of aircraft carriers in relation to naval operations, providing not only 'eyes' over the horizon, but potent new weapons that could be used to defend a fleet, or strike at the opposing fleet with torpedoes, armour-piercing

bombs, and even more devastating weapons. Japan, for example, used its famous Mitsubishi A6M Zero carrier based fighter as a flying bomb in the last, desperate stages of the war, loading the aircraft with bombs for *kamikaze* attacks in which, initially, volunteer pilots flew their aircraft directly at the target. Used in this way for the first time in late 1944, five Zeros sank the escort carrier US *St Lo*.

Since the end of the war methods have been developed to allow advanced fighter/strike aircraft to operate from carriers, simplified by the adoption of a through deck configuration, steam catapults for launching and improved arrester gear. It is of considerable interest that the highly sophisticated McDonnell Douglas F–4 Phantom II, mentioned earlier in this chapter as entering service with the USAF, was in fact designed for and is used by the United States Navy and Marine Corps. Its performance was such during USN evaluation that the USAF showed interest in the F–4 for use in a ground attack role and large numbers are in service for that purpose, as well as being used as multi-role fighters and for reconnaissance. Additionally, the Phantom serves also in naval and air force versions with several other nations.

The first pure jet aircraft to operate from the deck of an aircraft carrier was the British de Havilland

Left: Blackburn's Buccaneer was developed to a Royal Navy requirement for a low level strike aircraft. Below: Taxiing with wings folded, and air brakes still deployed, the Supermarine Scimitar was the Royal Navy's first single seat supersonic fighter. Right: Lockheed's SR–71 strategic reconnaissance aircraft, capable of Mach 3 plus performance in level flight, which demonstrated its capability by flying from New York to London (5584 km : 3470 miles) in 1 h 54 min 56.4 sec to take part in the 1974 Farnborough Air Show.

Sea Vampire, a first deck landing on 3 December 1945 being followed by 15 takeoffs and landings in the ensuing two days. Since that time many first class turbojet powered aircraft have served with the British Fleet Air Arm, the very first in FAA first line squadron service being the Supermarine Attacker which, contrary to the F–4's USN/USAF relationship, was first designed for service with the RAF.

The original role envisaged for the military aircraft was reconnaissance, and as we have already discovered the 'eyes in the sky' could do this job so well that they brought about the evolution of the entire family of aircraft types for differing military tasks.

The reconnaissance role has never ceased to be absolutely vital, and just before the beginning of World War 2 the German Colonel-General Baron von Fritsch had predicted: 'The next war will be won by the military organization with the most efficient photographic reconnaissance.' Certainly, this comment was to become true, for America and Britain developed airborne reconnaissance and photographic interpretation to new levels of capability and provided, in particular, advance knowledge of completely unexpected German radar installations and, at a later stage of the war, knowledge of the new V weapons being created by Hitler's scientists and engineers.

At that early period there was little effort made to produce a highly efficient reconnaissance aircraft. The usual practice was to take the most advanced fighter aircraft at any one time, strip it of every piece of equipment that was not vital for the new role, and then install the essential cameras. Thus, the wartime skies over Europe became a regular haunt for PR (photo reconnaissance) versions of the American P–38 Lightning, P–51 Mustang, British de Havilland Mosquito, Supermarine Spitfire and German Junkers Ju 88 and Messerschmitt Me 109.

Special reconnaissance versions of many postwar high performance aircraft have been built, capable not only of 'seeing' with highly developed cameras, but which also use special sensors to sniff out enemy troops concealed in jungle terrain, listen for submarines deep beneath the sea, or enemy troops and convoys moving by dark. They also use infrared sensors to pinpoint enemy armour and aircraft which have been concealed by camouflage techniques. In addition, special high altitude aircraft have been developed to overfly enemy territory seeking general information but, in particular, to keep an eye on activities associated with the manufacture and test of nuclear weapons, as well as the development of ballistic missiles.

Perhaps the most famous of such aircraft was the Lockheed U–2, designed by C.L. 'Kelly' Johnson, who aimed to produce an aircraft which would fly so high that there would be little chance of intercepting it. It had to be light in weight, which was achieved by using the lightest possible materials, and so that its jet engine could operate as economically as possible the aircraft had large area wings which meant that, once airborne and at high altitude, it would be able to glide for long periods of flight. It carried sophisticated cameras designed by Dr Edwin Land, known to the public for his Land or Polaroid instant picture cameras, which had such remarkable resolution that they could pinpoint golf balls on a putting green 16,800 m (55,000 ft) below. It was one of these U–2 aircraft, piloted by Francis Gary Powers, that was brought down over Sverdlovsk in Russia, on 1 May 1960, causing a serious rift in international relations. Subsequently, U–2s brought back reconnaissance pictures taken over Cuba which first alerted the world to the fact that defensive surface to air missile (SAM) sites were being erected. Defensive though these sites were, it was considered desirable to keep a close eye on future developments. More U–2 pictures, on 14 October 1962, confirmed that there were then in existence medium range ballistic missile sites, with their weapons trained against the United States. And when President John F. Kennedy let the Soviet Union know that a missile attack from Cuba against any nation would bring massive nuclear retaliation, it

Above: A vivid impression of inverted formation aerobatics.

Above: McDonnell Douglas F–15A Eagle fixed wing fighter. **Left:** Grumman F–14 Tomcat 'swing wing' fighter for carrier based operation.

was only a short time before the sites were dismantled. Reconnaissance aircraft had demonstrated their capability and importance, preventing a situation that could have led to war.

Mention has been made of the rocket engined Bell X–1 research aircraft, but it is only fair to record that Germany had introduced a rocket powered interceptor, the Messerschmitt Me 163 Komet, into operational service on 16 August 1944. They achieved very limited success by the war's end, due particularly to fuel shortages and inadequate pilot training.

Rocket motors have been the power plant of two very interesting postwar aircraft. First is the North American X–15A–2 research aircraft, which was used to continue investigations into the problems of high speed flight. When its programme terminated, it had been flown at a maximum speed of 7297 km/h (4534 mph: Mach 6.72), and to a height of 108 km

(67.08 miles). The other is the Martin Marietta X–24 lifting-body research aircraft that has been used in both powered and unpowered form to investigate the problems associated with manoeuvring manned re-entry vehicles able to fly as spacecraft in orbit, re-enter and fly in earth's atmosphere like conventional aircraft and land on an airport type runway. If this does not seem familiar it really ought to, for most of you who read this will have seen on television the first test flights of NASA's full size space shuttle orbiter, bearing the appropriate name *Enterprise*.

It is research and development projects of this kind which make possible new generation combat aircraft recently in—or soon to enter—squadron service. America has several exciting aircraft, including the Grumman F–14 Tomcat for the US Navy. This has a 'swing wing', to permit carrier based usage, which is computer controlled for optimum performance. General Dynamics and McDonnell Douglas have built the F–16 and F–15 Eagle fighters respectively. The former has a 'fly by wire' control system, in which a multi-path electrical system operates the flight controls. The F–15 Eagle has advanced electronics and an engine which lets it climb like a rocket. The European consortium Panavia has produced the Tornado multi-role combat aircraft, and Russia has evolved the formidable MiG–25 with a speed capability in excess of Mach 3.

Light and special purpose planes

The pioneers who dreamed of free, powered flight, had no thoughts of using the aeroplane as a weapon of war. The possibility that, one day, aircraft and weapons would be developed which could destroy our civilization would have seemed to them an abhorrent vision. This can be emphasized by the words of Orville Wright who at the end of World War 1 was to comment: 'What a dream it was; what a nightmare it has become.'

Happily there is another side to the coin, part of which we have explored already in the development of civil transport aircraft which carry millions of passengers annually for business and pleasure. It is the section of aviation which the pioneers regarded as their goal to which we now turn, the development of light aircraft for purely peaceful uses.

Immediately prior to World War 1 the general trend of aviation was of a sporting nature, such as the 'Round Britain' air race of 1911, the first Schneider Trophy contest at Monaco in 1913, and the third British Aerial Derby, won by an American pilot less than two months before the outbreak of war in 1914. And, of course, individuals owned and flew aeroplanes just for pleasure. Flying was an expensive hobby which only the wealthy could enjoy, but that is not to say that aviation did not appeal to the masses of people who would run excitedly to watch any aeroplane in the sky.

One of the British pioneers was Claude Grahame-White, a businessman who acquired a tract of land at Hendon, northwest of London, which he converted into an aerodrome complete with flying school. There, in the immediate prewar years, he presented flying displays to which Londoners flocked in their thousands. Similar meetings were held in other European countries, especially in France and Germany, but there was not the same enthusiasm from the public in America.

When the war ended there were some significant changes in the aviation scene. To start with, many thousands of young men had learned to fly and, even during the fears and horrors of war, had discovered those magical moments when man and machine blend as one, achieving the long held dream of flying like a bird. Not surprisingly, very many of them still wanted to fly after the war, but it was a difficult desire to fulfil because there were few opportunities for pilots in civil aviation; air forces were cut to a minute fraction of their wartime strength and private flying was still expensive.

There was a wide appreciation of the fact that in the years ahead there would be an enormous expansion of aviation, in a large variety of categories, but in those immediate postwar years there was a need to enthuse the general public of all nations. It was not too difficult for an ex-service pilot to acquire a government surplus aircraft at very moderate cost, and there was a demand for two seat trainers or light aircraft which could be used to carry one or more passengers who, for a moderate fee, were given their first taste of flight as a passenger, the 'plane flying from any reasonably level field.

From such small beginnings originated the postwar era of the 'barnstormers', in all nations of the world, gradually indoctrinating the general public to the fact that they, too, could fly. Among the ranks of these pilots were the stuntmen, who would thrill the crowds that gathered to watch them with such hair raising feats as wing walking, perhaps with an acrobat dangling from the aircraft's undercarriage, or with two aircraft flying so close that a man—or woman—could scramble from one to the other. And after such a demonstration they would offer cheap flights to the crowd, earning a precarious living in this way.

There were more serious efforts to make the public air-minded, a number of pilots joining together to form a flying circus with the emphasis on getting large numbers of the crowd into the air. Typical of this was the British pilot Alan (later Sir Alan) Cobham's Air Display circuses which in the period 1932–36 carried nearly a million passengers.

Even before that date, however, there had been a very significant event which was to have great future implications for the light aeroplane: Geoffrey de Havilland designed a light, robust and easy to fly two seater, the D.H.60 Moth, which flew in prototype form for the first time on 22 February 1925. Soon after, the British Secretary of State for Air authorized five flying clubs to be equipped with Moths, each receiving a subsidy so that growing numbers of people could learn to fly. Other clubs followed, not only in Britain but all over the world, using the D.H.60 Moth, and the more important Gipsy engined D.H. 60G Gipsy Moth which superseded it in 1927. Whereas previous light aircraft had been built in very small quantities, the D.H.60 was built in dozens, the D.H.60G in hundreds. Large numbers went to Australia, and it is perhaps with that country, more

Completely out of context, in relation to date, is the Missionary Aviation Fellowship, formed in London in 1945 under the leadership of Murray Kendon who had been a pilot in the Royal New Zealand Air Force. This organization followed the lead of the Christian Airmen's Missionary Fellowship inaugurated in America during the previous year, but both the US and British foundations now use the MAF title. Using lightplanes the missionaries spread Christianity in practical form to needy and under-privileged people, the initial contact bringing medical supplies to treat the sick and alleviate suffering, or

Left: The Grumman American Cheetah is typical of the beautifully finished lightplanes which grace general aviation in the 1970s.

than any other, that the Gipsy Moth has its closest associations. The first England–Australia flight by a woman was achieved by Amy Johnson in a Gipsy Moth, and so was the flight of Francis (later Sir Francis) Chichester, remembered for a unique feat of navigation on a flight from New Zealand to Australia in 1931.

These achievements, and many others made in new and steadily improving light planes, did much to impress the non flying majority that aviation was becoming a safe means of travel. Furthermore, with the passing of the years, it is now possible to look back and see how important this branch of general aviation has become, far removed from air races and the pioneer flights which once made the headlines.

Especially important has been the contribution of aviation towards the alleviation of suffering, and in this context one must pinpoint the work of the late Rev. Dr John Flynn, who was the founder of what is today Australia's Royal Flying Doctor Service which was established in 1928. It began with the use of a QANTAS loaned D.H.50 four seater together with a pilot, and on 15 May 1928 a surgeon, K. St Vincent Welch, became the world's first flying doctor. In 1934 the D.H.50 was replaced by D.H.83 Fox Moths, which had an open cockpit for the pilot and a small enclosed cabin forward. Two years later radio-telephones were introduced and the Flying Doctor Service—granted the prefix Royal by H.M. Queen Elizabeth in 1955—was off on a sound footing. This Service, in the 'seventies, was flying more than 804,000 km (half a million miles) each year and still, predominantly, using lightplanes.

food to allay the pangs of starvation.

Lightplanes began another important task for man-kind as long ago as 1925, when American cotton crops were being decimated by boll weevils. One C.E. Woolman had the idea that it might be possible to distribute a pesticide from the air, for in no other way would it be practical to attempt any form of control over such vast areas. Thus was born Huff-Daland Dusters Inc., which not only controlled the boll weevil in 1925, but was the foundation of agricultural aviation which is now worldwide, and of ever growing importance. Control of pests and fungus diseases which threaten growing crops is no longer the primary requirement of such aircraft, but it has been shown that vast areas of land can be made productively fertile by spreading fertilizers from the air. While this is no new thought, there are enormous tracts of land which it would be impossible to dust economically without the use of aircraft. The Soviet Union has the world's largest fleet of agricultural aircraft operated by the national airline Aeroflot, with America a close second. Such aircraft have demonstrated their importance by, for example, playing a key role in the control of the desert locust in Africa. There is every indication that in the years ahead this very specialized type of light aircraft will prove a vital weapon against the growing problem of world hunger. Light aircraft also have a function in a related part of ecology, namely the distribution and preservation of wild life, and many nations now have organizations which work on a full time basis in this field. Observation from aircraft makes it possible to count populations of animals and large birds, keep an eye on distributions and migrations, and the US Wild Life Service even uses aircraft to re-establish fish populations in lakes which, for one reason or another, have fallen way below normal.

Aircraft have shown their importance in countries which have large areas of timber. Canada and America are typical examples of nations with vast woodlands which are frequently affected by long periods of dry weather. Under such conditions a carelessly thrown cigarette, a spark from a picnic fire, or a lightning strike, can create a forest fire of frightening proportions. The coming of the aeroplane has provided a

has enabled single aircraft, fighting a fire within easy reach of a suitable water supply, to make more than 100 drops—more than half a million litres of water—in a single day.

It will be appreciated that World War 2 did even more than the previous major conflict to make both men and women interested in learning to fly. But in the early days of peace there were no large numbers of aircraft available at giveaway prices which were suitable for the private pilot. This brought a large expansion of trade in the manufacture of private aircraft, and companies like Beech, Cessna and Piper

Left: The Cessna light-plane is but one of many which have been converted for use as floatplanes. Left below: From an earlier era, the de Havilland D.H.80A Puss Moth of 1930 vintage. Below: This British designed Taylor Monoplane was built in the USA.

valuable tool to spot fires; a platform from which to direct operations; a means of transporting a first-line fire-fighting team known as the 'smoke jumpers', who descend near to the base of the fire by parachute; and a means of deluging the area of the fire with water. If caught early enough, this latter technique has proved capable of extinguishing a forest fire; more generally, however, it serves to contain the blaze or slow its spread until conventional fire fighters can reach the scene.

The Canadian company of Canadair Ltd has built about 60 CL–215 amphibians for use primarily as water bombers, these being able to carry 5455 litres (1200 Imp. gallons) of water or chemical retardants. Water can be scooped from the surface of a lake, river or the sea, and the latest models can refill their water tanks in ten seconds. This sort of performance

in America have grown from small to large in the process. The products of these companies, and others like them around the world, are beautifully finished, well designed and safe aircraft, available in a wide range of sizes, and with equipment which can be very basic or with advanced electronics for navigation, communications, and weather alerting, as well as to provide automatic control and stability augmentation. Unfortunately, such aircraft were, and still are, comparatively expensive.

This brought an upsurge in home built aircraft, especially in America, where in the early 1950s the Experimental Aircraft Association was established to help individuals by guiding them along the right lines of constructional techniques, and by giving help and advice with the many problems that can face the builder at home. Today the EAA has branches—

Moving into a larger class of general aviation aircraft the Cessna Skymaster (this page, below) has an unusual pull-push twin engine arrangement. This page, bottom: the graceful and reliable Cessna 180 of which about 6000 have been built, mostly for private use.

Right: Designed and built by de Havilland Canada, this very colourful example of the DHC–6 Twin Otter can seat up to 20 passengers. Its economy, and rugged reliability, has meant that it is used for utility purposes by many air forces.

which it calls chapters—in many countries of the world, and has done a great deal to foster the spread of a kind of private flying which the very first pioneers would have understood and applauded.

We have, of course, seen many way out designs: very often they were on the way out even before they took to the air. There have also been some really remarkable aircraft evolved, especially from France and the United States. Men like Marcel Jurca and Claude Piel in France have evolved some classic designs of which plans are available to amateur constructors. The same applies to James Bede and Ladislao Pazmany in America, and there are exciting designs with some almost research type aircraft, like Peter Garrison's Melmoth and 'Bert' Rutan's Variviggen. There are also aircraft right at the other end of the scale, cleverly designed to embody very lightweight and cheap structures, such as the Birdman TL–1 and Hovey Whing Ding II, which have empty weights of 45 kg (100 lb) and 55.5 kg (123 lb) respectively. It is, perhaps, unfair to pinpoint just a few of these aircraft which are being built and flown by enthusiasts, but there are so many available currently that they warrant a book on their own.

So far we have looked mainly at aeroplanes which operate from land surfaces but, unlike large commercial aircraft, there is a fairly wide variety of seaplanes, mini flying boats and amphibians making up the ranks of lightplanes. There are also many ski equipped aircraft, able to operate from and to snow and ice covered surfaces, and often performing important work in desolate and mountainous regions. While there are some designs suitable for home construction, the majority are slightly larger aircraft which can be made to perform what may seem strange tasks. In fact they are doing jobs which only an aeroplane can carry out practically, or economically, proving yet again the enormous contribution that modern aviation makes towards the world in which we live.

Lightplanes like those (above) have innumerable uses: G–AZIK is a Piper Seneca 6/7-seat utility aircraft; the British Airports Authority Rockwell Shrike Commander a workhorse. The biplanes (right) are constructed especially for aerobatics.

In winter sports regions, such as the Swiss Alps, ski equipped lightplanes are used for rescue operations at quite high altitudes, carrying the rescued to safety or hospital in a fraction of the time taken by a conventional mountain rescue team. And in many areas of the world where snow is commonplace, light ski planes are extensively used for a variety of day to day tasks, as well as for sport and pleasure. In much the same way, floatplanes and lightweight flying boats have a useful job to do, especially in countries like Canada which has large numbers of inland water surfaces that can be used by aircraft of this type. A typical usage in Canada is that which operates, in effect, a 'bus service', with small amphibian flying boats such as the Grumman Goose or Widgeon picking up and putting down passengers along routes that use lakes, rivers and coastal towns as their 'airports'. But almost certainly the biggest use of ski and floatplanes in the 1970s is in America's rapidly developing 49th state of Alaska, the nature of the terrain and climate making the aeroplane a vital means of communication for people, as well as a maid of all work so far as supplies and materials are concerned.

Another country which has a number of ski/float planes in regular service is New Zealand, and Mount Cook Airlines and Southern Scenic Air Services both operate these types of aircraft to carry tourists to some of the country's beauty spots which, by any other form of transport, could not be included in the itineraries of holidaymakers with just two or three weeks' vacation.

Way back in the years between the wars, when it was still necessary to work hard to make the public

Left and below: Canadair's CL–215 amphibian used primarily as a water bomber for fire fighting, can be hydrant filled on the ground or can, while skimming a water surface, scoop up enough water to fill its tanks in 10 seconds. Overleaf: (inset) Dassault Falcon 20 twin turbo-fan executive transport, and (full-page) the Hawker Siddeley HS 125 designed to fulfil the same role as 'executive jets'.

air minded, air races were just one means of attracting a large following of spectators. This served another important purpose in developing the type of lightplanes and the engines which powered them. Races such as the international Schneider Trophy contests not only aroused tremendous interest, but played a significant role in the evolution of high powered and reliable piston engines. The same kind of process of improvement had occurred with the motor car at an earlier date, the pounding and stresses of competition highlighting the weaknesses of design and/or construction. The primary growth of air racing came initially in America, for climatic, geographic and economic reasons, but interest in competition between lightplanes has increased rapidly in recent years, particularly in pylon racing where similar aircraft are involved. Such races, to the accompaniment of a great

deal of excitement and noise, prove most thrilling as pilots, rather than machines, compete in a trial of ability.

The skill of a pilot, so far as the general public is concerned, has been linked since the early days of flight by his efficiency in performing aerobatic manoeuvres with an aircraft. It began in 1913 when Lt Nesterov of the Imperial Russian Army 'looped the loop', as it was at first called. His feat was soon copied by pilots of other nations, and inverted flight and 'falling leafs' became the stock in trade of any young airman seeking to impress. The cut and thrust of air combat added new aerobatics—such as the Immelmann turn—and the postwar flying displays, especially of the kind staged by the RAF at Hendon, provided a new spectacle for the public. Since then air shows have featured some wonderful displays by service formation-aerobatic teams, in recent years flying high performance training or combat aircraft which are not strictly within our category of lightplanes. Today, service aerobatic teams such as the French *Patrouille de France*, Italian *Frecce Tricolori*, and Britain's *Red Arrows* are known internationally. Solo aerobatics have also become international with the introduction of a world aerobatic championship in 1960. Since then the capability of the competitors has been raised almost to a classic art form, using highly specialized and stressed aircraft.

The major growth in the development and production of light aircraft has been in the field of business and commuter airline flying. Growing international competition in the marketing of high technology products has made it essential for major companies to send a team of salesmen and technical specialists to the customer; and since speed is often vital in signing up a contract, the aeroplane has assumed growing importance in this role. Commuter airlines have grown rapidly for a number of reasons other than greater acceptance of air travel by the public. National airlines, most of which had developed from small beginnings, found that an economic necessity to equip with aircraft suited for their major, and often international, routes meant it was no longer profitable to offer services over local, short range routes. The commuter airlines moved in to close the gap, and as major airports became sited further away from cities, the commuter could often come up with a faster city to city service than a jet service between major airports necessitating road or rail connections at both ends.

In this chapter we have by no means covered the whole scope of general aviation which, in the main, is served by small/medium aircraft. We have not touched on air survey, traffic control nor fishery protection, to mention but three. Clearly, however, the aeroplane has a most important function in our modern world.

OH-FFA

139

PT-DTY

Helicopters and jump jets

The helicopter is an aircraft that has no conventional fixed wing like those which we have looked at in the pages of this book so far. Instead, it has two or more aerofoil surfaces mounted to rotate above the aircraft's fuselage to provide both lift and propulsion. There is also another form of rotary winged aircraft, namely the autogyro, which uses its rotating aerofoil surfaces to develop lift, and is propelled through the air by a conventional power plant.

The helicopter's history stretches back as fas as the Italian artist/engineer Leonardo da Vinci who, about 1490, sketched the design of a helical screw rotary winged flying machine. Perhaps his interest had been aroused by the string-launched flying-propeller toys which were then popular in Europe, but it was two Frenchmen, Launoy and Bienvenu, who mounted two propellers on a short rod, using a bow and bowstring device to rotate them, who demonstrated the first self propelled helicopter model in April 1784. Twelve years later Sir George Cayley produced an improved version of the Launoy/Bienvenu model, using the same bowstring propulsion device, but providing two four-blade rotors, each comprising four feathers stuck into a cork. Then there is a gap of nearly fifty years, until 1842, when W.H. Phillips in Britain demonstrated a model helicopter, its rotor propelled by a tiny pressure jet at the tip of each blade.

Not until 1907 was it possible to achieve vertical flight in a heavier than air aircraft, and on 13 November Frenchman Paul Cornu piloted a helicopter of his own design in brief vertical flight. This gave proof that the rotary wing was practical, but Cornu's machine could only rise or descend vertically, he had no means of controlling the two rotors to give any degree of horizontal flight. But the principle of cyclic pitch control, which would make this possible, had already been suggested by an Italian, G.A. Crocco, and was demonstrated to be practical by the Danish aviation pioneer J.C.H. Ellehammer when he flew a full size helicopter in 1912.

At about the same time that Paul Cornu was experimenting with his twin rotor helicopters, the young Igor Sikorsky, in Russia, was building his first helicopter. This had twin contra rotating rotors, to cancel out the torque of a single rotor, but this and his succeeding design, first flown in 1910, were inadequately powered, and Sikorsky concentrated then upon the development of fixed wing aircraft.

The war of 1914–18 then interrupted further progress, as there was the need to develop and produce in quantity practical fixed wing aircraft, rather than waste effort on research projects. In the postwar years the first helicopter to demonstrate successfully the application of cyclic pitch control was built by an Argentinian, the Marquis de Pescara, working in France and Spain in the period 1919–25. He, however, was unable to overcome satisfactorily the problems caused by rotor torque.

The most important early work, beginning in 1920, was carried out by a young Spaniard, Juan de la Cierva. He was concerned to develop a successful autogyro, having discovered that an unpowered rotor was not only free from the problem of torque, but if once set in rotation prior to flight would continue to autorotate, and would provide sufficient lift to replace the conventional fixed wing of an aircraft. Since the rotor would autorotate, failure of the engine/propeller combination providing forward motion would mean only that the autogyro would continue in flight and make a safe, if steep, descent. It offered new standards of flight safety and de la Cierva was determined to succeed.

For his initial experiments, de la Cierva used a conventional fixed wing aircraft with a single unpowered rotor mounted on a pylon so that it was above the aircraft's fuselage. A rope wound round the rotor shaft enabled assistants to start the rotor spinning, and as the aircraft taxied forward it continued to autorotate. Unfortunately, when he attempted to take off, the machine did not become airborne, but tipped over on its side. When further attempts ended in the same way, de la Cierva realized that he was faced with a fundamental problem associated with the rotary wing. He discovered that when the entire aircraft was moving forward, the rotor blades

Above: The Bell Model 47 was in continuous production for more than 25 years; those shown above are Sioux helicopters serving with the British army. Left: The Sikorsky S–65A is in a very different category, being a heavy assault transport which can accommodate up to 55 troops.

Three very differing rotary winged aircraft are shown
on this page. Inset, immediately above: An early
autogyro with unpowered auto-rotating wings. Inset,
top: A Bell Model 47 single rotor helicopter, serving
with the British army under the name Sioux. The large
twin-rotor Boeing Vertol Chinook was not only
invaluable for supply operations as illustrated, in
Vietnam, but in this theatre lifted out some 6000
disabled aircraft and transported them to repair bases.

Top left: Typical use of helicopter in forward battle areas, putting down troops and their supplies. Left: A Sikorsky S–64 Skycrane with Universal Military Pod attached, which can carry 45 troops and be adapted in the field for a variety of uses. Above: The Fairey Rotodyne compound helicopter prototype, which had a large powered rotor for vertical take off and landing, and propellors for conventional horizontal flight. Right: A civil version of the Bell Model 47 helicopter, which received the United States CAA's first helicopter Approved Type Certificate on 8 March 1946.

advancing into the airstream were developing more lift than those retreating from the airstream, tipping the rotor, and hence the aircraft over. It took him a considerable time to design a rotor to overcome this problem, providing each blade with a hinge to allow a degree of up and down movement. Thus, as the advancing blade gains lift it rises, and in so doing loses some of its effectiveness by virtue of the blade's design. The retreating blade drops, and in so doing gains lift, with the result that the rotor becomes self balancing. For the first time an aircraft with a single rotor became practical, but this was true only for an unpowered rotor; the problem relating to torque—which could be overcome by using two powered and contra rotating rotors—still had to be resolved before a practical single rotor helicopter could become reality.

Juan de la Cierva called the aircraft which he built *Autogiros*, and by 1928 they were being built under licence in America and Britain. His aircraft were of

little practical value, however, with a rotary wing replacing a fixed wing. They did, however, provide an additional safety feature in the event of a power plant failure, so that he had achieved what he had set out to do. Ironically, de la Cierva was killed in a landing accident in a fixed wing aircraft. He is remembered, however, for the flapping hinge rotor which made practical helicopters possible, and the first of these began to emerge in the late 1930s. They included twin rotor helicopters by Breguet in France, Focke-Wulf in Germany and Weir in Britain: twin rotors because no one had solved the torque problem of a single rotor helicopter.

This was to be the great achievement of Igor Sikorsky, by then a naturalized American, who designed a small vertical tail rotor, carried on an extended boom, to provide a sideways thrust to offset the torque of the main rotor. His VS–300 helicopter prototype, which made its first tethered flight on 14 September 1939, had not entirely resolved the

problems of control, and it was not until 1942 that it could be acclaimed the world's first thoroughly practical single rotor helicopter.

Simultaneous with the late development work on the VS–300, Sikorsky was building an experimental XR–4 helicopter for the USAAF. Very similar to the VS–300, it differed primarily by having side by side seating for a two man crew, and the skeleton structure of the earlier helicopter was faired in. It also had a far more powerful engine, a 123 kW (165 hp) Warner engine, and following a first flight in January 1942, flew in easy stages from Stratford, Connecticut to Dayton, Ohio, completing in the process the world's first long distance helicopter cross country flight. In all 100 R–4s were built in various designations, and were the first helicopters to enter service, being used for evaluation by the US Army Air Force, Navy and Coast Guard, and by the British Air Force and Navy.

From this small beginning has grown the enormous family of helicopters, manufactured in all shapes and sizes by companies all over the world, because from the initial service evaluation of that first production helicopter came an appreciation of the fact that the world had suddenly acquired a completely new kind of vehicle. Aeroplane though it was, it could behave like no other aeroplane before it, for not only had it the ability to hover over a point, it could also fly backwards or sideways, and took off and landed vertically. This latter feature provided a virtual go anywhere capability, and helicopters soon began to demonstrate their potential. For military operations it was clear they could put down and pick up troops almost anywhere, as well as their arms, ammunition and supplies. Navies could use them to provide fast messengers or eyes in the sky for quite small vessels; they could act as watch dogs during carrier operations, and they could lift a pilot to safety if he was unfortunate enough to end up in the water. Civil helicopters showed that they, too, had the ability to rescue feckless people cut off by the tide, carried to sea on air beds or stranded on the cliffs as they took birds' eggs. They could also rescue those who were trapped on mountains, pick up injured seamen from vessels at sea, civilians stranded in floods, check power lines, help erect buildings, and carry lumber. There was very little they could not do, but in those early years of the 1940s it required an enormous amount of development to make them more reliable and capable of lifting bigger payloads. Then, on 25 June 1950, war broke out in Korea, and United Nations troops were soon involved in an attempt to prevent the escalation of this conflict into a major war. It provided a first opportunity to evaluate the helicopter in active service conditions, and it was not long before it was clear to all of the nations involved that this new vehicle was of immense importance. Not only was it invaluable for its ability to transport troops and supplies into otherwise completely inaccessible front line areas, but because it could lift

injured troops from forward positions and speed them to hospitals for treatment, it reduced the figure of death from wounds to the lowest ever recorded in military history. And not only could helicopters operate to anywhere, they could also operate from nowhere: in other words, they did not need long concrete runways and sophisticated installations.

This first appreciation of the real military potential resulted in a big demand for new and improved designs, and for helicopters designed to fulfil specific roles so that instead of just being ubiquitous and partially efficient, they could become specialized aircraft fulfilling particular roles in the most efficient way possible.

One of the problems was that they were not really economical to operate, except for military purposes when cost was not paramount. The first civil operators soon found that they had wedded themselves to a machine of frightening appetite for while these new

Above: Russia's Mil Mi–12 (V–12), seen first by Western observers at the 1971 Paris Air Show. The largest helicopter yet flown, it has a maximum take off weight of 105,000 kg (231,500 lb), and yet can demonstrate a maximum level speed of 260 km/h (161 mph). Right: Helicopter use in Korea and Vietnam showed that armed versions could be valuable in a close support role. Typical of those developed for this purpose is the Bell AH–1G HueyCobra, used also to escort bigger and slower helicopters. Armament comprises a six-barrel Minigun in a chin turret, and a variety of weapons can be carried beneath stub wings.

Messerschmitt-Bölkow-Blohm in Germany has developed a single rotor helicopter known as the MBB BO 105. It features a rigid rotor hub and has four flexible main rotor blades made of glassfibre. An anti-tank version has been built and it is this which is illustrated (left). Six Hot anti-tank missiles are carried and these are optically guided by a stabilized sight. A hit effectiveness of 90 per cent has been demonstrated in service trials. Inset is a view of the aircraft's controls and instruments.

craft were versatile they needed a lot of fuel and support to lift a very modest payload. Civil operators who pioneered helicopter passenger services, such as New York Airways in the US, Sabena in Belgium and British European Airways, soon discovered that they could not continue to operate without government subsidy. Relief came in the late 1950s with the introduction of gas turbine power plants, their much smaller size allowing them to be mounted outside of the fuselage, usually on top of the cabin, and so increasing the available internal space. In addition, they offered a much improved power/weight ratio, as well as considerably more power, and made the carriage of passengers a far more attractive proposition.

This sort of development has not been confined to the West, and the Soviet Union with its vast territories has found the all purpose nature of the helicopter of great importance. Not only has development followed the trends of the West, but Russia has proved also to be an innovative builder of rotary winged aircraft. First in service was the Mil Mi–4, which entered the ranks of the Red Air Force in 1953. Since then several thousands have been built, many equipped for an anti-submarine warfare (ASW) role, as well as serving with Aeroflot as 11–16 seat passenger aircraft, as an air ambulance and for agricultural dusting and/or spraying. In fact, Russia has built and has in production the massive Mil Mi–12 (V–12) helicopter, with twin rotors that each have a diameter of 35.00 m (114 ft 10 in) and which span 67.00 m (219 ft 10 in). It can take off vertically with a payload of 25,000 kg (55,000 lb) and serves with both the Red Air Force and Aeroflot in a heavy transport role.

At the other end of the scale are tiny personal autogyros, such as those designed and marketed by Russian born Igor Bensen in America. His B–8M, for example, was designed for home construction from a kit or plans. Its rotor is of 6.10 m (20 ft) diameter and a 53.5 kW (72 hp) engine drives a pusher propeller to speed the B–8M through the air at 137 km/h (85 mph).

The combination of more powerful turbines and the conventional flapping-hinge rotor soon pinpointed the fact that this rotor, rather like the propellers of fixed wing aircraft, had reached the peak of its development and was limiting speed and performance. Extensive research programmes were initiated by the major helicopter manufacturers to evolve improved rotors, leading to so called rigid rotors and new blades of improved aerodynamic section and constructed of advanced materials to give longer blade life. The rigid rotor is not, in fact, rigid but uses elastomeric materials to provide hingeless attachments for the blades, and these permit controlled flexibility, reduce drag from the rotor hub, and simplify maintenance.

For military use, rotor transmission systems have been evolved which can now have grease packed and sealed gear boxes: in the event of combat damage they have no oil to lose and can continue to operate for a limited period. To improve performance much work is being done to evolve compound helicopters, usually by the addition of a fixed wing to provide lift in forward flight that will relieve the propulsive rotor of load and permit faster flight. Designers are even investigating the possibility of evolving a rotor which can be folded after takeoff, permitting a fixed wing to support the aircraft in high speed flight. Other research is concerned with the development of new VTOL (vertical takeoff and landing) systems which will dispense with the rotary wing.

The Canadian company Canadair built a tilt wing aircraft which used large diameter propellers to provide vertical lift when the wing was tilted so that the propellers were horizontal. As the wing moved forward to a conventional setting there was a transition from vertical to horizontal flight, and Canadair's CL–84 has demonstrated hovering flight and a forward speed in excess of 483 km/h (200 mph). Bell, in America, has explored a different technique, the company's Model D2127 having four ducted fans, two of which were mounted at the tips of a foreplane, and two on the aft sited main wing. It has demonstrated forward speeds in excess of 412 km/h (255 mph), and sustained hovering flight at an altitude of 2445 m (8020 ft). Dornier, in Germany, has investigated the use of what are known as vectored-thrust engines to achieve VTOL performance. This type of engine, developed by Rolls-Royce Bristol, is of the turbofan variety. Air ducted from the tips of the fan is ejected through lateral nozzles which can be directed downward to provide lift, or rotated aft to provide propul-

sive thrust. The hot gases from the turbine are ejected through a similar pair of nozzles at the aft of the engine. Dornier used two of the engines in its Do 31 E research aircraft, plus eight lift jets, mounted four at each wing tip. This aircraft, designed as a transport to carry 36 fully equipped troops, has demonstrated a speed of over 513 km/h (319 mph).

Research to evolve an aircraft of this class in Britain began in the late 1950s with the development of the Rolls-Royce Bristol (then Bristol Aero-Engines) Pegasus vectored-thrust turbofan. Hawker Siddeley designed and built the prototype of a single-seat V/STOL (vertical/short takeoff and landing) reconnaissance/close support aircraft to use this engine, and this P.1127 (later named Kestrel), made its first transitions from vertical to horizontal flight, and

vice versa, in September 1961.

Since that time the Pegasus has been developed to produce considerably more thrust, the current Mk 103 version developing 95.6 kN (21,500 lb) static thrust. It is this engine which powers the Hawker Siddeley Harrier, the western world's only operational fixed-wing V/STOL strike fighter. It can take off vertically from a small forest clearing and, after transition to horizontal flight, can demonstrate a low-altitude speed of more than 1186 km/h (737 mph). The Harrier is a valuable combat aircraft, currently in service with the RAF; more than 100 were ordered by the US Marine Corps, with whom they serve under the designation AV–8A, and the Spanish Navy will have at least six, which will be called Matadors.

In little more than 35 years the VTOL aircraft has developed from the first tentative designs to a vehicle which fulfils a vital role in both civil and military use. At the heavy end of the scale transports carry troops, passengers and cargo; flying cranes can pick up damaged aircraft, carry out construction work, lift valuable timber in difficult logging operations. Helicopters have proved essential to the offshore exploration for gas and oil, and the subsequent production of much needed energy from these new fields. They can be potent, heavily armed killers in military usage but more importantly, they can perform errands of mercy and comfort in speed and safety.

Below: The Hawker Siddeley Harrier in typical front line usage. Overleaf: A Sikorsky–64 Skycrane shows the kind of delivery job of which modern heavy lift helicopters are capable.

Index

Page numbers in italics refer to illustration captions

ACKNOWLEDGMENTS

The publishers would like to thank the following organisations and individuals for their kind permission to reproduce the photographs in this book:

Air B.P. 9; Basil Arkell 96 above left and below; Chris Barker 24–25; Barnaby's Picture Library 94–95; The Boeing Company title, 31, 57; British Aircraft Corporation 65 below, 71 below; Camera Press 12–13, 15 below, 16–17; Elizabeth Photo Library (Jack Novak) 4–5; Mary Evans Picture Library 6; Expression 68–69; James Gilbert end papers, 15 above, 54–55, 82, 83 above, 83 below right, 86 right, 88 below; Hawker-Siddeley Aviation Limited 59, 90–91; Leslie Hunt 21 above; Robert Hunt Library 39 below; Imperial War Museum 18–19, 51 above; Howard Levy 16, 21 below, 80 below; Kenneth McDonough 27; Ministry of Defence 100–101; Kenneth Munson 88 above; Quantas Airways Limited 8, 10; John Rigby 63, 78–79; Ronan Picture Library 7; Brian M Service 65 above; Spectrum Colour Library 10–11, 35, 38 below, 93 above and below; J.W.R. Taylor 14, 22–23, 28–29, 32, 33 above and below, 34, 38 above, 40–41, 49, 50–51, 56 above and below, 58, 60–61, 60 below, 66, 67, 70, 71 above, 72–73, 76 above and below, 77, 80 above, 83 below left, 84 above and below, 85, 87, 96 above right, 97, 98 above and below, 99 above, 102.